ST. THOMAS AQUINAS

ST. THOMAS AQUINAS

BY

G. K. CHESTERTON

ISBN: 978-93-5128-890-9(PB)

First Published in 1933
Indian Reprint in 2017

Published by

Kalpaz Publications
C-30, Satyawati Nagar,
Delhi – 110052
E-mail: kalpaz@hotmail.com
Website: kalpazpublications.com
Ph.: +91-9212142040

CONTENTS

INTRODUCTORY NOTE 7

Chapter I
ON TWO FRIARS 9

Chapter II
THE RUNAWAY ABBOT 25

Chapter III
THE ARISTOTELIAN REVOLUTION 34

Chapter IV
A MEDITATION ON THE MANICHEES 51

Chapter V
THE REAL LIFE OF ST. THOMAS 64

Chapter VI
THE APPROACH TO THOMISM 77

Chapter VII
THE PERMANENT PHILOSOPHY 86

Chapter VIII
THE SEQUEL TO ST. THOMAS 98

INTRODUCTORY NOTE

This book makes no pretence to be anything but a popular sketch of a great historical character who ought to be more popular. Its aim will be achieved, if it leads those who have hardly even heard of St. Thomas Aquinas to read about him in better books. But from this necessary limitation certain consequences follow, which should perhaps be allowed for from the start.

First, it follows that the tale is told very largely to those who are not of the communion of St. Thomas; and who may be interested in him as I might be in Confucius or Mahomet. Yet, on the other hand, the very need of presenting a clean-cut outline involved its cutting into other outlines of thought, among those who may think differently. If I write a sketch of Nelson mainly for foreigners, I may have to explain elaborately many things that all Englishmen know, and possibly cut out, for brevity, many details that many Englishmen would like to know. But, on the other side, it would be difficult to write a very vivid and moving narrative of Nelson, while entirely concealing the fact that he fought with the French. It would be futile to make a sketch of St. Thomas and conceal the fact that he fought with heretics; and yet the fact itself may embarrass the very purpose for which it is employed. I can only express the hope, and indeed the confidence, that those who regard me as the heretic will hardly blame me for expressing my own convictions, and certainly not for expressing my hero's convictions. There is only one point upon which such a question concerns this very simple narrative. It is the conviction, which I have expressed once or twice in the course of it, that the sixteenth-century schism was really a belated revolt of the thirteenth-century pessimists. It was a back-wash of the old Augustinian Puritanism against the Aristotelian liberality. Without that, I could not place my historical figure in history. But the whole is meant only for a rough sketch of a figure in a landscape and not of a landscape with figures.

Second, it follows that in any such simplification I can hardly say much of the philosopher beyond showing that he had a philosophy. I have only, so to speak, given samples of that philosophy. Lastly, it follows that it is practically impossible to deal adequately with the theology. A lady I know picked up a book of selections from St. Thomas with a commentary; and began hopefully to read a section with the innocent heading, "The Simplicity of God." She then laid down the book with a sigh and said, "Well, if that's His simplicity, I wonder what His complexity is like." With all respect to that excellent Thomistic commentary. I have no desire to have this book laid down, at the very first glance, with a similar sigh. I have taken the view that the biography is an introduction to the philosophy, and that the philosophy is an introduction to the theology; and that I can only carry the reader just beyond the first stage of the story.

Third, I have not thought it necessary to notice those critics who, from time to time, desperately play to the gallery by reprinting paragraphs of medieval demonology in the hope of horrifying the modern public merely by an unfamiliar language. I have taken it for granted that educated men know that Aquinas and all his contemporaries, and all his opponents for centuries after, did believe in demons, and similar facts, but I have not thought them worth mentioning here, for the simple reason that they do not help to detach or distinguish the portrait. In all that, there was no disagreement between Protestant or Catholic theologians, for all the hundreds of years during which there was any theology; and St. Thomas is not notable as holding such views, except in holding them rather mildly. I have not discussed such matters, not because I have any reason to conceal them, but because they do not in any way personally concern the one person whom it is here my business to reveal. There is hardly room, even as it is, for such a figure in such a frame.

CHAPTER I

ON TWO FRIARS

Let me at once anticipate comment by answering to the name of that notorious character, who rushes in where even the Angels of the Angelic Doctor might fear to tread. Some time ago I wrote a little book of this type and shape on St. Francis of Assisi; and some time after (I know not when or how, as the song says, and certainly not why) I promised to write a book of the same size, or the same smallness on St. Thomas Aquinas. The promise was Franciscan only in its rashness; and the parallel was very far from being Thomistic in its logic. You can make a sketch of St. Francis: you could only make a plan of St. Thomas, like the plan of a labyrinthine city. And yet in a sense he would fit into a much larger or a much smaller book. What we really know of his life might be pretty fairly dealt with in a few pages; for he did not, like St. Francis, disappear in a shower of personal anecdotes and popular legends. What we know, or could know, or may eventually have the luck to learn, of his work, will probably fill even more libraries in the future than it has filled in the past. It was allowable to sketch St. Francis in an outline; but with St. Thomas everything depends on the filling up of the outline. It was even medieval in a manner to illuminate a miniature of the Poverello, whose very title is a diminutive. But to make a digest, in the tabloid manner, of the Dumb Ox of Sicily passes all digestive experiments in the matter of an ox in a tea-cup. But we must hope it is possible to make an outline of biography, now that anybody seems capable of writing an outline of history or an outline of anything. Only in the present case the outline is rather an outsize. The gown that could contain the colossal friar is not kept in stock.

I have said that these can only be portraits in outline. But the concrete contrast is here so striking, that even if we actually saw the two human figures in outline, coming over the hill in their friar's gowns, we should find that contrast even comic. It would be like seeing, even afar off, the silhouettes of Don Quixote and Sancho Panza, or of Falstaff and Master Slender. St. Francis was a lean and lively little man; thin as a thread and vibrant as a bowstring; and in his motions like an arrow from the bow. All his life was a series of plunges and scampers: darting after the beggar, dashing naked into the woods, tossing himself into the strange ship, hurling himself into the Sultan tent and offering to hurl himself into the fire. In appearance he must have been like a thin brown skeleton autumn leaf dancing eternally before the wind; but in truth it was he that was the wind.

St. Thomas was a huge heavy bull of a man, fat and slow and quiet; very mild and magnanimous but not very sociable; shy, even apart from the humility of holiness; and abstracted, even apart from his occasional and carefully concealed experiences of trance or ecstasy. St. Francis was so fiery and even fidgety that the ecclesiastics, before whom he appeared quite suddenly, thought he was a madman. St. Thomas was so stolid that the scholars, in the schools which he attended regularly, thought he was a dunce. Indeed, he was the sort of schoolboy, not unknown, who would much rather be thought a dunce than have his own dreams invaded, by more active or animated dunces. This external contrast extends to almost every point in the two personalities. It was the paradox of St. Francis that while he was passionately fond of poems, he was rather distrustful of books. It was the outstanding fact about St. Thomas that he loved books and lived on books; that he lived the very life of the clerk or scholar in *The Canterbury Tales*, who would rather have a hundred books of Aristotle and his philosophy than any wealth the world could give him. When asked for what he thanked God most, he answered simply, "I have understood every page I ever read." St. Francis was very vivid in his poems and rather vague in his documents; St. Thomas devoted his whole life to documenting whole systems of Pagan and Christian literature; and occasionally wrote a hymn like a man taking a holiday. They saw the same problem from different angles, of simplicity and subtlety; St. Francis thought it would be enough to pour out his heart to the Mohammedans, to persuade them not to worship Mahound. St. Thomas bothered his head with every hair-splitting distinction and deduction, about the Absolute or the Accident, merely to prevent them from misunderstanding Aristotle. St. Francis was the son of a shopkeeper, or middle class trader; and while his whole life was a revolt against the mercantile life of his father, he retained none the less, something of the quickness and social adaptability which makes the market hum like a hive. In the common phrase, fond as he was of green fields, he did not let the grass grow under his feet. He was what American millionaires and gangsters call a live wire. It is typical of the mechanistic moderns that, even when they try to imagine a live thing, they can only think of a mechanical metaphor from a dead thing. There is such a thing as a live worm; but there is no such thing as a live wire. St. Francis would have heartily agreed that he was a worm; but he was a very live worm. Greatest of all foes to the go-getting ideal, he had certainly abandoned getting, but he was still going. St. Thomas, on the other hand, came out of a world where he might have enjoyed leisure, and he remained one of those men whose labour has something of the placidity of leisure. He was a hard worker, but nobody could possibly mistake him for a hustler. He had something indefinable about him, which marks those who work when they need not work. For he was by birth a gentleman of a great house, and such repose can remain as a habit, when it is no longer a motive. But in him it was expressed only in its most amiable elements; for instance, there was possibly something of it in his effortless courtesy and patience. Every saint is a man before he is a saint; and a saint may be made of every sort or kind of man; and most of us will choose between these different types according to our different tastes. But I will confess that, while the romantic glory of St. Francis has lost nothing of its glamour for me, I have in later years grown to feel almost as much affection, or in some aspects even more, for this man who unconsciously inhabited a large heart and a large head, like one inheriting a large house, and exercised there an equally generous if rather more absent-minded hospitality. There are moments when St. Francis, the most unworldly man who ever walked the world, is almost too efficient for me.

St. Thomas Aquinas has recently reappeared, in the current culture of the colleges and the salons, in a way that would have been quite startling even ten years ago. And the mood that has concentrated on him is doubtless very different from that which popularised St. Francis quite twenty years ago.

The Saint is a medicine because he is an antidote. Indeed that is why the saint is often a martyr; he is mistaken for a poison because he is an antidote. He will generally be found restoring the world to sanity by exaggerating whatever the world neglects, which is by no means always the same element in every age. Yet each generation seeks its saint by instinct; and he is not what the people want, but rather what the people need. This is surely the very much mistaken meaning of those words to the first saints, "Ye are the salt of the earth," which caused the Ex-Kaiser to remark with all solemnity that his beefy Germans were the salt of the earth; meaning thereby merely that they were the earth's beefiest and therefore best. But salt seasons and preserves beef, not because it is like beef; but because it is very unlike it. Christ did not tell his apostles that they were only the excellent people, or the only excellent people, but that they were the exceptional people; the permanently incongruous and incompatible people; and the text about the salt of the earth is really as sharp and shrewd and tart as the taste of salt. It is because they were the exceptional people, that they must not lose their exceptional quality. "If salt lose its savour, wherewith shall it be salted?" is a much more pointed question than any mere lament over the price of the best beef. If the world grows too worldly, it can be rebuked by the Church; but if the Church grows too worldly, it cannot be adequately rebuked for worldliness by the world.

Therefore it is the paradox of history that each generation is converted by the saint who contradicts it most. St. Francis had a curious and almost uncanny attraction for the Victorians; for the nineteenth century English who seemed superficially to be most complacent about their commerce and their common sense. Not only a rather complacent Englishman like Matthew Arnold, but even the English Liberals whom he criticised for their complacency, began slowly to discover the mystery of the Middle Ages through the strange story told in feathers and flames in the hagiographical pictures of Giotto. There was something in the story of St. Francis that pierced through all those English qualities which are most famous and fatuous, to all those English qualities which are most hidden and human: the secret softness of heart; the poetical vagueness of mind; the love of landscape and of animals. St. Francis of Assisi was the only medieval Catholic who really became popular in England on his own merits. It was largely because of a subconscious feeling that the modern world had neglected those particular merits. The English middle classes found their only missionary in the figure, which of all types in the world they most despised; an Italian beggar.

So, as the nineteenth century clutched at the Franciscan romance, precisely because it had neglected romance, so the twentieth century is already clutching at the Thomist rational theology, because it has neglected reason. In a world that was too stolid, Christianity returned in the form of a vagabond; in a world that has grown a great deal too wild, Christianity has returned in the form of a teacher of logic. In the world of Herbert Spencer men wanted a cure for indigestion; in the world of Einstein they want a cure for vertigo. In the first case, they dimly perceived the fact that it was after a long fast that St. Francis sang the Song of the Sun and the praise of the fruitful earth. In the second case, they already dimly perceived that, even if they only want to understand Einstein, it is necessary first to understand the use of the understanding. They begin to see that, as the eighteenth century thought itself the age of reason, and the nineteenth century thought itself the age of common sense, the twentieth century cannot as yet even manage to think itself anything but the age of uncommon nonsense. In those conditions the world needs a saint; but above all, it needs a philosopher. And these two cases do show that the world, to do it justice, has an instinct for what it needs. The earth was really very flat, for those Victorians who most vigorously repeated that it was round, and Alverno of the Stigmata stood up as a single mountain in the plain. But the earth is an earthquake, a ceaseless and apparently endless earthquake, for the moderns for whom Newton has been scrapped along with Ptolemy. And for them there is something more steep and even incredible than a mountain; a piece of really solid ground; the level of the level-headed man. Thus in our time the two saints have appealed to two generations, an age of romantics and an age of sceptics; yet in their own age they were doing the same work; a work that has changed the world.

Again, it may be said truly that the comparison is idle, and does not fit in well even as a fancy: since the men were not properly even of the same generation or the same historic moment. If two friars are to be presented as a pair of Heavenly Twins, the obvious comparison is between St. Francis and

St. Dominic. The relations of St. Francis and St. Thomas were, at nearest, those of uncle and nephew; and my fanciful excursus may appear only a highly profane version of "Tommy make room for your uncle." For if St. Francis and St. Dominic were the great twin brethren, Thomas was obviously the first great son of St. Dominic, as was his friend Bonaventure of St. Francis. Nevertheless, I have a reason (indeed two reasons) for taking as a text the accident of two title-pages; and putting St. Thomas beside St. Francis, instead of pairing him off with Bonaventure the Franciscan. It is because the comparison, remote and perverse as it may seem, is really a sort of short cut to the heart of history; and brings us by the most rapid route to the real question of the life and work of St. Thomas Aquinas. For most people now have a rough but picturesque picture in their minds of the life and work of St. Francis of Assisi. And the shortest way of telling the other story is to say that, while the two men were thus a contrast in almost every feature, they were really doing the same thing. One of them was doing it in the world of the mind and the other in the world of the worldly. But it was the same great medieval movement; still but little understood. In a constructive sense, it was more important than the Reformation. Nay, in a constructive sense, it was the Reformation.

About this medieval movement there are two facts that must first be emphasised. They are not, of course, contrary facts, but they are perhaps answers to contrary fallacies. First, in spite of all that was once said about superstition, the Dark Ages and the sterility of Scholasticism, it was in every sense a movement of enlargement, always moving towards greater light and even greater liberty. Second, in spite of all that was said later on about progress and the Renaissance and forerunners of modern thought, it was almost entirely a movement of orthodox theological enthusiasm, unfolded from within. It was *not* a compromise with the world, or a surrender to heathens or heretics, or even a mere borrowing of external aids, even when it did borrow them. In so far as it did reach out to the light of common day, it was like the action of a plant which by its own force thrusts out its leaves into the sun; not like the action of one who merely lets daylight into a prison.

In short, it was what is technically called a Development in doctrine. But there seems to be a queer ignorance, not only about the technical, but the natural meaning of the word Development. The critics of Catholic theology seem to suppose that it is not so much an evolution as an evasion; that it is at best an adaptation. They fancy that its very success is the success of surrender. But that is not the natural meaning of the word Development. When we talk of a child being well-developed, we mean that he has grown bigger and stronger with his own strength; not that he is padded with borrowed pillows or walks on stilts to make him look taller. When we say that a puppy develops into a dog, we do not mean that his growth is a gradual compromise with a cat; we mean that he becomes more doggy and not less. Development is the expansion of all the possibilities and implications of a doctrine, as there is time to distinguish them and draw them out; and the point here is that the enlargement of medieval theology was simply the full comprehension of that theology. And it is of primary importance to realise this fact first, about the time of the great Dominican and the first Franciscan, because their tendency, humanistic and naturalistic in a hundred ways, was truly the development of the supreme doctrine, which was also the dogma of all dogmas. It is in this that the popular poetry of St. Francis and the almost rationalistic prose of St. Thomas appear most vividly as part of the same movement. There are both great growths of Catholic development, depending upon external things only as every living and growing thing depends on them; that is, it digests and transforms them, but continues in its own image and not in theirs. A Buddhist or a Communist might dream of two things which simultaneously eat each other, as the perfect form of unification. But it is not so with living things. St. Francis was content to call himself the Troubadour of God; but not content with the God of the Troubadours. St. Thomas did not reconcile Christ to Aristotle; he reconciled Aristotle to Christ.

Yes; in spite of the contrasts that are as conspicuous and even comic as the comparison between the fat man and the thin man, the tall man and the short: in spite of the contrast between the vagabond and the student, between the apprentice and the aristocrat, between the book-hater and the book-lover, between the wildest of all missionaries and the mildest of all professors, the great fact of medieval history is that these two great men were doing the same great work; one in the study and the other in the street. They were not bringing something new into Christianity; in the sense of something heathen or heretical into Christianity; on the contrary, they were bringing Christianity into Christendom. But they were bringing it back against the pressure of certain historic tendencies, which had hardened into habits in many great schools and authorities in the Christian Church; and they were using tools and weapons which seemed to many people to be associated with heresy or heathenry. St. Francis used Nature much as St. Thomas used Aristotle; and to some they seemed to be using a Pagan goddess and a Pagan sage. What they were really doing, and especially what St. Thomas was really doing, will form the main matter of these pages; but it is convenient to be able to compare him from the first with a more popular saint; because we may thus sum up the substance of it in the most popular way. Perhaps it would sound too paradoxical to say that these two saints saved us from Spirituality; a dreadful doom. Perhaps it may be misunderstood if I say that St. Francis, for all his love of animals, saved us from being Buddhists; and that St. Thomas, for all his love of Greek philosophy, saved us from being Platonists. But it is best to say the truth in its simplest form; that they both reaffirmed the Incarnation, by bringing God back to earth.

This analogy, which may seem rather remote, is really perhaps the best practical preface to the philosophy of St. Thomas. As we shall have to consider more closely later on, the purely spiritual or mystical side of Catholicism had very much got the upper hand in the first Catholic centuries; through the genius of Augustine, who had been a Platonist, and perhaps never ceased to be a Platonist; through the transcendentalism of the supposed work of the Areopagite; through the Oriental trend of the later Empire and something Asiatic about the almost pontifical kinghood of Byzantium; all these things weighed down what we should now roughly call the Western element; though it has as good a right to be called the Christian element: since its common sense is but the holy familiarity of the word made flesh. Anyhow, it must suffice for the moment to say that theologians had somewhat stiffened into a sort of Platonic pride in the possession of intangible and untranslatable truths within; as if no part of their wisdom had any root anywhere in the real world. Now the first thing that Aquinas did, though by no means the last, was to say to these pure transcendentalists something substantially like this.

"Far be it from a poor friar to deny that you have these dazzling diamonds in your head, all designed in the most perfect mathematical shapes and shining with a purely celestial light; all there, almost before you begin to think, let alone to see or hear or feel. But I am not ashamed to say that I find my reason fed by my senses; that I owe a great deal of what I think to what I see and smell and taste and handle; and that so far as my reason is concerned, I feel obliged to treat all this reality as real. To be brief, in all humility, I do not believe that God meant Man to exercise only that peculiar, uplifted and abstracted sort of intellect which you are so fortunate as to possess: but I believe that there is a middle field of facts which are given by the senses to be the subject matter of the reason; and that in that field the reason has a right to rule, as the representative of God in Man. It is true that all this is lower than the angels; but it is higher than the animals, and all the actual material objects Man finds around him. True, man also can be an object; and even a deplorable object. But what man has done man may do; and if an antiquated old heathen called Aristotle can help me to do it I will thank him in all humility."

Thus began what is commonly called the appeal to Aquinas and Aristotle. It might be called the appeal to Reason and the Authority of the Senses. And it will be obvious that there is a sort of popular parallel to it in the fact that St. Francis did not only listen for the angels, but also listened to the birds. And before we come to those aspects of St. Thomas that were very severely intellectual, we may note that in him as in St. Francis there is a preliminary practical element which is rather moral; a sort of good and straightforward humility; and a readiness in the man to regard even himself in some ways as an animal; as St. Francis compared his body to a donkey. It may be said that the contrast holds everywhere, even in zoological metaphor, and that if St. Francis was like that common or garden donkey who carried Christ into Jerusalem, St. Thomas, who was actually compared to an ox, rather resembled that Apocalyptic monster of almost Assyrian mystery; the winged bull. But again, we must not let all that can be contrasted eclipse what was common; or forget that neither of them would have been too proud to wait as patiently as the ox and ass in the stable of Bethlehem.

There were of course, as we shall soon see, many other much more curious and complicated ideas in the philosophy of St. Thomas; besides this primary idea of a central common sense that is nourished by the five senses. But at this stage, the point of the story is not only that this was a Thomist doctrine, but that it is a truly and eminently Christian doctrine. For upon this point modern writers write a great deal of nonsense; and show more than their normal ingenuity in missing the point. Having assumed without argument, at the start, that all emancipation must lead men away from religion and towards irreligion, they have just blankly and blindly forgotten what is the outstanding feature of the religion itself.

It will not be possible to conceal much longer from anybody the fact that St. Thomas Aquinas was one of the great liberators of the human intellect. The sectarians of the seventeenth and eighteenth centuries were essentially obscurantists, and they guarded an obscurantist legend that the Schoolman was an obscurantist. This was wearing thin even in the nineteenth century; it will be impossible in the twentieth. It has nothing to do with the truth of their theology or his; but only with the truth of historical proportion, which begins to reappear as quarrels begin to die down. Simply as one of the facts that bulk big in history, it is true to say that Thomas was a very great man who reconciled religion with reason, who expanded it towards experimental science, who insisted that the senses were the windows of the soul and that the reason had a divine right to feed upon facts, and that it was the business of the Faith to digest the strong meat of the toughest and most practical of pagan philosophies. It is a fact, like the military strategy of Napoleon, that Aquinas was thus fighting for all that is liberal and enlightened, as compared with his rivals, or for that matter his successors and supplanters. Those who, for other reasons, honestly accept the final effect of the Reformation will none the less face the fact, that it was the Schoolman who was the Reformer; and that the later Reformers were by comparison reactionaries. I use the word not as a reproach from my own stand-point, but as a fact from the ordinary modern progressive standpoint. For instance, they riveted the mind back to the literal sufficiency of the Hebrew Scriptures; when St. Thomas had already spoken of the Spirit giving grace to the Greek philosophies. He insisted on the social duty of works; they only on the spiritual duty of faith. It was the very life of the Thomist teaching that Reason can be trusted: it was the very life of Lutheran teaching that Reason is utterly untrustworthy.

Now when this fact is found to be a fact, the danger is that all the unstable opposition will suddenly slide to the opposite extreme. Those who up to that moment have been abusing the Schoolman as a dogmatist will begin to admire the Schoolman as a Modernist who diluted dogma. They will hastily begin to adorn his statue with all the faded garlands of progress, to present him as a man in advance of his age, which is always supposed to mean in agreement with our age; and to load him with the unprovoked imputation of having produced the modern mind. They will discover his attraction, and somewhat hastily assume that he was like themselves, because he was attractive. Up to a point this is pardonable enough; up to a point it has already happened in the case of St. Francis. But it would not go beyond a certain point in the case of St. Francis. Nobody, not even a Freethinker like Renan or Matthew Arnold, would pretend that St. Francis was anything but a devout Christian, or had any other original motive except the imitation of Christ. Yet St. Francis also had that liberating and humanising effect upon religion; though perhaps rather on the imagination than the intellect. But nobody says that St. Francis was loosening the Christian code, when he was obviously tightening it; like the rope round his friar's frock. Nobody says he merely opened the gates to sceptical science, or sold the pass to heathen humanism, or looked forward only to the Renaissance or met the Rationalists half way. No biographer pretends that St. Francis, when he is reported to have opened the Gospels at random and read the great texts about Poverty, really only opened the *Aeneid* and practised the *Sors Virgiliana* out of respect for heathen letters and learning. No historian will pretend that St. Francis wrote *The Canticle of the Sun* in close imitation of a Homeric Hymn to Apollo or loved birds because he had carefully learned all the trick of the Roman Augurs.

In short, most people, Christian or heathen, would now agree that the Franciscan sentiment was primarily a Christian sentiment, unfolded from within, out of an innocent (or, if you will, ignorant) faith in the Christian religion itself. Nobody, as I have said, says that St. Francis drew his primary inspiration from Ovid. It would be every bit as false to say that Aquinas drew his primary inspiration from Aristotle. The whole lesson of his life, especially of his early life, the whole story of his childhood and choice of a career, shows that he was supremely and directly devotional; and that he passionately loved the Catholic worship long before he found he had to fight for it. But there is also a special and clinching instance of this which once more connects St. Thomas with St. Francis. It seems to be strangely forgotten that both these saints were in actual fact imitating a Master, who was not Aristotle let alone Ovid, when they sanctified the senses or the simple things of nature; when St. Francis walked humbly among the beasts or St. Thomas debated courteously among the Gentiles.

Those who miss this, miss the point of the religion, even if it be a superstition; nay, they miss the very point they would call most superstitious. I mean the whole staggering story of the God-Man in the Gospels. A few even miss it touching St. Francis and his unmixed and unlearned appeal to the Gospels. They will talk of the readiness of St. Francis to learn from the flowers or the birds as something that can only point onward to the Pagan Renaissance. Whereas the fact stares them in the face; first, that it points backwards to the New Testament, and second that it points forward, if it points to anything, to the Aristotelian realism of the *Summa* of St. Thomas Aquinas. They vaguely imagine that anybody who is humanising divinity must be paganising divinity without seeing that the humanising of divinity is actually the strongest and starkest and most incredible dogma in the Creed. St. Francis was becoming more like Christ, and not merely more like Buddha, when he considered the lilies of the field or the fowls of the air; and St. Thomas was becoming more of a Christian, and not merely more of an Aristotelian, when he insisted that God and the image of God had come in contact through matter with a material world. These saints were, in the most exact sense of the term, Humanists; because they were insisting on the immense importance of the human being in the theological scheme of things. But they were not Humanists marching along a path of progress that leads to Modernism and general scepticism; for in their very Humanism they were affirming a dogma now often regarded as the most superstitious Superhumanism. They were strengthening that staggering doctrine of Incarnation, which the sceptics find it hardest to believe. There cannot be a stiffer piece of Christian divinity than the divinity of Christ.

This is a point that is here very much to the point; that these men became more orthodox, when they became more rational or natural. Only by being thus orthodox could they be thus rational and natural. In other words, what may really be called a liberal theology was unfolded from within, from out of the original mysteries of Catholicism. But that liberality had nothing to do with liberalism; in fact it cannot even now coexist with liberalism [(footnote) I use the word liberalism here in the strictly limited theological sense, in which Newman and other theologians use it. In its popular political sense, as I point out later, St. Thomas rather tended to be a Liberal, especially for his time]. The matter is so cogent, that I will take one or two special ideas of St. Thomas to illustrate what I mean. Without anticipating the elementary sketch of Thomism that must be made later, the following points may be noted here.

For instance, it was a very special idea of St. Thomas that Man is to be studied in his whole manhood; that a man is not a man without his body, just as he is not a man without his soul. A corpse is not a man; but also a ghost is not a man. The earlier school of Augustine and even of Anselm had rather neglected this, treating the soul as the only necessary treasure, wrapped for a time in a negligible napkin. Even here they were less orthodox in being more spiritual. They sometimes hovered on the edge of those Eastern deserts that stretch away to the land of transmigration where the essential soul may pass through a hundred unessential bodies; reincarnated even in the bodies of beasts or birds. St. Thomas stood up stoutly for the fact that a man's body is his body as his mind is his mind; and that he can only be a balance and union of the two. Now this is in some ways a naturalistic notion, very near to the modern respect for material things; a praise of the body that might be sung by Walt Whitman or justified by D H. Lawrence: a thing that might be called Humanism or even claimed by Modernism. In fact, it may be Materialism; but it is the flat contrary of Modernism. It is bound up, in the modern view, with the most monstrous, the most material, and therefore the most miraculous of miracles. It is specially connected with the most startling sort of dogma, which the Modernist can least accept; the Resurrection of the Body.

Or again, his argument for Revelation is quite rationalistic; and on the other side, decidedly democratic and popular. His argument for Revelation is not in the least an argument against Reason. On the contrary, he seems inclined to admit that truth could be reached by a rational process, if only it were rational enough; and also long enough. Indeed, something in his character, which I have called elsewhere optimism, and for which I know no other approximate term, led him rather to exaggerate the extent to which all men would ultimately listen to reason. In his controversies, he always assumes that they will listen to reason. That is, he does emphatically believe that men can be convinced by argument; when they reach the end of the argument. Only his common sense also told him that the argument never ends. I might convince a man that matter as the origin of Mind is quite meaningless, if he and I were very fond of each other and fought each other every night for forty years. But long before he was convinced on his deathbed, a thousand other materialists could have been born, and nobody can explain everything to everybody. St. Thomas takes the view that the souls of all the ordinary hard-working and simple-minded people are quite as important as the souls of thinkers and truth-seekers; and he asks how all these people are possibly to find time for the amount of reasoning that is needed to find truth. The whole tone of the passage shows both a respect for scientific enquiry and a strong sympathy with the average man. His argument for Revelation is not an argument against Reason; but it is an argument for Revelation. The *conclusion* he draws from it is that men must receive the highest moral truths in a miraculous manner; or most men would not receive them at all. His arguments are rational and natural; but his own deduction is all for the supernatural; and, as is common in the case of his argument, it is not easy to find any deduction except his own deduction. And when we come to that, we find it is something as simple as St. Francis himself could desire; the message from heaven; the story that is told out of the sky; the fairytale that is really true.

It is plainer still in more popular problems like Free Will. If St. Thomas stands for one thing more than another, it is what may be called subordinate sovereignties or autonomies. He was, if the flippancy may be used, a strong Home Ruler. We might even say he was always defending the independence of dependent things. He insisted that such a thing could have its own rights in its own region. It was his attitude to the Home Rule of the reason and even the senses; "Daughter am I in my father's house; but mistress in my own." And in exactly this sense he emphasised a certain dignity in Man, which was sometimes rather swallowed up in the purely theistic generalisations about God. Nobody would say he wanted to divide Man from God; but he did want to distinguish Man from God. In this strong sense of human dignity and liberty there is much that can be and is appreciated now as a noble humanistic liberality. But let us not forget that its upshot was that very Free Will, or moral responsibility of Man, which so many modern liberals would deny. Upon this sublime and perilous liberty hang heaven and hell, and all the mysterious drama of the soul. It is distinction and not division; but a man *can* divide himself from God, which, in a certain aspect, is the greatest distinction of all.

Again, though it is a more metaphysical matter, which must be mentioned later, and then only too slightly, it is the same with the old philosophical dispute about the Many and the One. Are things so different that they can never be classified: or so unified that they can never be distinguished? Without pretending to answer such questions here, we may say broadly that St. Thomas comes down definitely on the side of Variety, as a thing that is real as well as Unity. In this, and questions akin to this, he often departs from the great Greek philosophers who were sometimes his models; and entirely departs from the great Oriental philosophers who are in some sense his rivals. He seems fairly certain that the difference between chalk and cheese, or pigs and pelicans, is not a mere illusion, or dazzle of our bewildered mind blinded by a single light; but is pretty much what we all feel it to be. It may be said that this is mere common sense; the common sense that pigs are pigs; to that extent related to the earthbound Aristotelian common sense; to a human and even a heathen common sense. But note that here again the extremes of earth and heaven meet. It is also connected with the dogmatic Christian idea of the Creation; of a Creator who created pigs, as distinct from a Cosmos that merely evolved them.

In all these cases we see repeated the point stated at the start. The Thomist movement in metaphysics, like the Franciscan movement in morals and manners, was an enlargement and a liberation, it was emphatically a growth of Christian theology from within; it was emphatically *not* a shrinking of Christian theology under heathen or even human influences. The Franciscan was free to be a friar, instead of being bound to be a monk. But he was more of a Christian, more of a Catholic, even more of an ascetic. So the Thomist was free to be an Aristotelian, instead of being bound to be an Augustinian. But he was even more of a theologian; more of an orthodox theologian; more of a dogmatist, in having recovered through Aristotle the most defiant of all dogmas, the wedding of God with Man and therefore with Matter. Nobody can understand the greatness of the thirteenth century, who does not realise that it was a great growth of new things produced by a living thing. In that sense it was really bolder and freer than what we call the Renaissance, which was a resurrection of old things discovered in a dead thing. In that sense medievalism was not a

Renascence, but rather a Nascence. It did not model its temples upon the tombs, or call up dead gods from Hades. It made an architecture as new as modern engineering; indeed it still remains the most modern architecture. Only it was followed at the Renaissance by a more antiquated architecture. In that sense the Renaissance might be called the Relapse. Whatever may be said of the Gothic and the Gospel according to St. Thomas, they were not a Relapse. It was a new thrust like the titanic thrust of Gothic engineering; and its strength was in a God who makes all things new.

In a word, St. Thomas was making Christendom more Christian in making it more Aristotelian. This is not a paradox but a plain truism, which can only be missed by those who may know what is meant by an Aristotelian, but have simply forgotten what is meant by a Christian. As compared with a Jew, a Moslem, a Buddhist, a Deist, or most obvious alternatives, a Christian *means* a man who believes that deity or sanctity has attached to matter or entered the world of the senses. Some modern writers, missing this simple point, have even talked as if the acceptance of Aristotle was a sort of concession to the Arabs; like a Modernist vicar making a concession to the Agnostics. They might as well say that the Crusades were a concession to the Arabs as say that Aquinas rescuing Aristotle from Averrhoes was a concessions to the Arabs. The Crusaders wanted to recover the place where the body of Christ had been, because they believed, rightly or wrongly, that it was a Christian place. St. Thomas wanted to recover what was in essence the body of Christ itself; the sanctified body of the Son of Man which had become a miraculous medium between heaven and earth. And he wanted the body, and all its senses, because he believed, rightly or wrongly, that it was a Christian thing. It might be a humbler or homelier thing than the Platonic mind that is why it was Christian. St. Thomas was, if you will, taking the lower road when he walked in the steps of Aristotle. So was God, when He worked in the workshop of Joseph.

Lastly, these two great men were not only united to each other but separated from most of their comrades and contemporaries by the very revolutionary character of their own revolution. In 1215, Dominic Guzman, the Castilian, founded an Order very similar to that of Francis; and, by a most curious coincidence of history, at almost exactly the same moment as Francis. It was directed primarily to preaching the Catholic philosophy to the Albigensian heretics; whose own philosophy was one of the many forms of that Manicheanism with which this story is much concerned. It had its roots in the remote mysticism and moral detachment of the East; and it was therefore inevitable that the Dominicans should be rather more a brotherhood of philosophers, where the Franciscans were by comparison a brotherhood of poets. For this and other reasons, St. Dominic and his followers are little known or understood in modern England; they were involved eventually in a religious war which followed on a theological argument; and there was something in the atmosphere of our country, during the last century or so, which made the theological argument even more incomprehensible than the religious war. The ultimate effect is in some ways curious; because St. Dominic, even more than St. Francis, was marked by that intellectual independence, and strict standard of virtue and veracity, which Protestant cultures are wont to regard as specially Protestant. It was of him that the tale was told, and would certainly have been told more widely among us if it had been told of a Puritan, that the Pope pointed to his gorgeous Papal Palace and said, "Peter can no longer say 'Silver and gold have I none;'" and the Spanish friar answered, "No, and neither can he now say, 'Rise and walk.'"

Thus there is another way in which the popular story of St. Francis can be a sort of bridge between the modern and medieval world. And it is based on that very fact already mentioned: that St. Francis and St. Dominic stand together in history as having done the same work, and yet are divided in English popular tradition in the most strange and startling way. In their own lands they are like Heavenly Twins, irradiating the same light from heaven, seeming sometimes to be two saints in one halo, as another order depicted Holy Poverty as two knights on one horse. In the legends of our own land, they are about as much united as St. George and the Dragon. Dominic is still conceived as an Inquisitor devising thumbscrews; while Francis is already accepted as a humanitarian deploring mousetraps. It seems, for instance, quite natural to us, and full of the same associations of flowers and starry fancies, that the name of Francis should belong to Francis Thompson. But I fancy it would seem less natural to call him Dominic Thompson; or find that a man, with a long record of popular sympathies and practical tenderness to the poor, could bear such a name as Dominic Plater. It would sound as if he had been called Torquemada Thompson.

Now there must be something wrong behind this contradiction; turning those who were allies at home into antagonists abroad. On any other question, the fact would be apparent to common sense. Suppose English Liberals or Free-Traders found that, in remote parts of China, it was generally held that Cobden was a cruel monster but Bright a stainless saint. They would think there was a mistake somewhere. Suppose that American Evangelicals learned that in France or Italy, or other civilizations impenetrable by Moody and Sankey, there was a popular belief that Moody was an angel but Sankey a devil; they would guess that there must be a muddle somewhere. Some other later accidental distinction must have cut across the main course of a historical tendency. These parallels are not so fantastic as they may sound. Cobden and Bright have actually been called "child-torturers," in anger at their alleged callousness about the evils amended by the Factory Acts; and some would call the Moody and Sankey sermon on Hell a hellish exhibition. All that is a matter of opinion; but both men held the same sort of opinion, and there must be a blunder in an opinion that separates them so completely. And of course there is a complete blunder in the legend about St. Dominic. Those who know anything about St. Dominic know that he was a missionary and not a militant persecutor; that his contribution to religion was the Rosary and not the Rack; that his whole career is meaningless, unless we understand that his famous victories were victories of persuasion and not persecution. He did believe in the justification of persecution; in the sense that the secular arm could repress religious disorders. So did everybody else believe in persecution; and none more than the elegant blasphemer Frederick II who believed in nothing else. Some say he was the first to burn heretics; but anyhow, he thought it was one of his imperial privileges and duties to persecute heretics. But to talk as if Dominic did nothing but persecute heretics, is like blaming Father Matthew, who persuaded millions of drunkards to take a temperance pledge, because the accepted law sometimes allowed a drunkard to be arrested by a policeman. It is to miss the whole point; which is that this particular man had a genius for conversion, quite apart from compulsion. The real difference between Francis and Dominic, which is no discredit to either of them, is that Dominic did happen to be confronted with a huge campaign for the conversion of heretics, while Francis had only the more subtle task of the conversion of human beings. It is an old story that, while we may need somebody like Dominic to convert the heathen to Christianity, we are in even greater need of somebody like Francis, to convert the Christians to Christianity. Still, we must not lose sight of St. Dominic's special problem, which was that of dealing with a whole population, kingdoms and cities and countrysides, that had drifted from the Faith and solidified into strange and abnormal new religions. That he did win back masses of men so deceived, merely by talking and preaching, remains an enormous triumph worthy of a colossal trophy. St. Francis is called humane because he tried to convert Saracens and failed; St. Dominic is called bigoted and besotted because he tried to convert Albigensians and succeeded. But we happen to be in a curious nook or corner of the hills of history, from which we can see Assisi and the Umbrian hills, but are out of sight of the vast battle-field of the Southern Crusade; the miracle of Muret and the greater miracle of Dominic, when the roots of the Pyrenees and the shores of the Mediterranean saw defeated the Asiatic despair.

But there is an earlier and more essential link between Dominic and Francis, which is more to the immediate purpose of this book. They were in later times bracketed in glory because they were in their own time bracketed in infamy; or at least in unpopularity. For they did the most unpopular thing that men can do; they started a popular movement. A man who dares to make a direct appeal to the populace always makes a long series of enemies—beginning with the populace. In proportion as the poor begin to understand that he means to help and not hurt them, the solid classes above begin to close in, resolved to hinder and not help. The rich, and even the learned, sometimes feel not unreasonably that the thing will change the world, not only in its worldliness or its worldly wisdom, but to some extent perhaps in its real wisdom. Such a feeling was not unnatural in this case; when we consider, for instance, St. Francis's really reckless attitude about rejecting books and scholarship; or the tendency that the Friars afterwards showed to appeal to the Pope in contempt of local bishops and ecclesiastical officers. In short, St. Dominic and St. Francis created a Revolution, quite as popular and unpopular as the French Revolution. But it is very hard today to feel that even the French Revolution was as fresh as it really was. The Marseillaise once sounded like the human voice of the volcano or the dance-tune of the earthquake, and the kings of the earth trembled. some fearing that the heavens might fall; some fearing far more that justice might be done. The Marseillaise is played today at diplomatic dinner-parties, where smiling monarchs meet beaming millionaires, and is rather less revolutionary than "Home Sweet Home." Also, it is highly pertinent to recall, the modern revolutionists would now call the revolt of the French Jacobins insufficient, just as they would call the revolt of the Friars insufficient. They would say that neither went far enough; but many, in their own day, thought they went very much too far. In the case of the Friars, the higher orders of the State, and to some extent even of the Church, were profoundly shocked at such a loosening of wild popular preachers among the people. It is not at all easy for us to feel that distant events were thus disconcerting and even disreputable. Revolutions turn into institutions; revolts that renew the youth of old societies in their turn grow old; and the past, which was full of new things, of splits and innovations and insurrections, seems to us a single texture of tradition.

But if we wish for one fact that will make vivid this shock of change and challenge, and show how raw and ragged, how almost rowdy in its reckless novelty, how much of the gutter and how remote from refined life, this experiment of the Friars did really seem to many in its own day, there is here a very relevant fact to reveal it. It shows how much a settled and already ancient Christendom did feel it as something like the end of an age; and how the very roads of the earth seem to shake under the feet of the new and nameless army; the march of the Beggars. A mystic nursery rhyme suggests the atmosphere of such a crisis: "Hark, hark, the dogs do bark; the Beggars are coming to town." There were many towns that almost fortified themselves against them and many watchdogs of property and rank did really bark, and hark loudly, when those Beggars went by; but louder was the singing of the Beggars who sang their Canticle to the Sun, and louder the baying of the Hounds of Heaven; the *Domini canes* of the medieval pun; the Dogs of God. And if we would measure how real and rending seemed that revolution, what a break with the past, we can see it in the first and most extraordinary event in the life of St. Thomas Aquinas.

CHAPTER II

THE RUNAWAY ABBOT

Thomas Aquinas, in a strange and rather symbolic manner, sprang out of the very centre of the civilised world of his time; the central knot or coil of the powers then controlling Christendom. He was closely connected with all of them; even with some of them that might well be described as destroying Christendom. The whole religious quarrel, the whole international quarrel, was for him, a family quarrel. He was born in the purple, almost literally on the hem of the imperial purple; for his own cousin was the Holy Roman Emperor. He could have quartered half the kingdoms of Europe on his shield — if he had not thrown away the shield. He was Italian and French and German and in every way European. On one side, he inherited from the energy that made the episode of the Normans, whose strange organising raids rang and rattled like flights of arrows in the corners of Europe and the ends of the earth; one flight of them following Duke William far northward through the blinding snows to Chester; another treading in Greek and Punic footsteps through the island of Sicily to the gates of Syracuse. Another bond of blood bound him to the great Emperors of the Rhine and Danube who claimed to wear the crown of Charlemagne; Red Barbarossa, who sleeps under the rushing river, was his great uncle, and Frederick II, the Wonder of the World, his second cousin, and yet he held by a hundred more intimate ties to the lively inner life, the local vivacity, the little walled nations and the thousand shrines of Italy. While inheriting this physical kinship with the Emperor, he maintained far more firmly his spiritual kinship with the Pope. He understood the meaning of Rome, and in what sense it was still ruling the world; and was not likely to think that the German Emperors of his times any more than the Greek Emperors of a previous time, would be able to be really Roman in defiance of Rome. To this cosmopolitan comprehensiveness in his inherited position, he afterwards added many things of his own, that made for mutual understanding among the peoples, and gave him something of the character of an ambassador and interpreter. He travelled a great deal; he was not only well known in Paris and the German universities, but he almost certainly visited England; probably he went to Oxford and London; and it has been said that we may be treading in the footsteps of him and his Dominican companions, whenever we go down by the river to the railway-station that still bears the name of Black-friars. But the truth applies to the travels of his mind as well as his body. He studied the literature even of the opponents of Christianity much more carefully and impartially than was then the fashion; he really tried to understand the Arabian Aristotelianism of the Moslems; and wrote a highly humane and reasonable treatise on the problem of the treatment of the Jews. He always attempted to look at everything from the inside; but he was certainly lucky in having been born in the inside of the state system and the high politics of his day. What he thought of them may perhaps be inferred from the next passage in his history.

St. Thomas might thus stand very well for the International Man, to borrow the title of a modern book. But it is only fair to remember that he lived in the International Age; in a world that was international in a sense not to be suggested in any modern book, or by any modern man. If I remember right, the modern candidate for the post of International Man was Cobden, who was an almost abnormally national man, a narrowly national man; a very fine type, but one which can hardly be imagined except as moving between Midhurst and Manchester. He had an international policy and he indulged in international travel; but if he always remained a national person, it was because he remained a normal person; that is normal to the nineteenth century. But it was not so in the thirteenth century. There a man of international influence, like Cobden, could be also almost a man of international nationality. The names of nations and cities and places of origin did not connote that deep division that is the mark of the modern world. Aquinas as a student was nicknamed the ox of Sicily, though his birthplace was near Naples, but this did not prevent the city of Paris regarding him as simply and solidly as a Parisian, because he had been a glory of the Sorbonne, that it proposed to bury his bones when he was dead. Or take a more obvious contrast with modern times. Consider what is meant in most modern talk by a German Professor. And then realise that the greatest of all German Professors, Albertus Magnus, was himself one of the glories of the University of Paris; and it was in Paris that Aquinas supported him. Think of the modern German Professor being famous throughout Europe for his popularity when lecturing in Paris.

Thus, if there was war in Christendom, it was international war in the special sense in which we speak of international peace. It was not the war of two nations; but the war of two internationalisms: of two World States: the Catholic Church and the Holy Roman Empire. The political crisis in Christendom affected the life of Aquinas at the start in one sharp disaster, and afterwards in many indirect ways. It had many elements; the Crusades; the embers of the Albigensian pessimism over which St. Dominic had triumphed in argument and Simon de Montfort in arms; the dubious experiment of an Inquisition which started from it; and many other things. But, broadly speaking, it is the period of the great duel between the Popes and the Emperors, that is the German Emperors who called themselves Holy Roman Emperors, the House of Hohenstaufen. The particular period of the life of Aquinas, however, is entirely overshadowed by the particular Emperor who was himself more an Italian than a German; the brilliant Frederick II who was called the Wonder of the World. It may be reminded, in passing, that Latin was the most living of languages at this time, and we often feel a certain weakness in the necessary translation. For I seem to have read somewhere that the word used was stronger than the Wonder of the World; that his medieval title was *Stupor Mundi*, which is more exactly the Stupefaction of the World. Something of the sort may be noted later of philosophical language, and the weakness of translating a word like *Ens* by a word like Being. But for the moment the parenthesis has another application; for it might well be said that Frederick did indeed stupefy the world; that there was something stunning and blinding about the blows he struck at religion, as in that blow which almost begins the biography of Thomas Aquinas. He may also be called stupefying in another sense; in that his very brilliancy has made some of his modern admirers very stupid.

For Frederick II is the first figure, and that a rather fierce and ominous figure, who rides across the scene of his cousin's birth and boyhood: a scene of wild fighting and of fire. And it may be allowable to pause for a parenthesis upon his name, for two particular reasons: first that his romantic reputation, even among modern historians, covers and partly conceals the true background of the times and second that the tradition in question directly involves the whole status of St. Thomas Aquinas. The nineteenth century view, still so strangely called the modern view by many moderns, touching such a man as Frederick II was well summed up by some solid Victorian, I think by Macaulay; Frederick was "a statesman in an age of Crusaders; a philosopher in an age of monks." It may be noted that the antithesis invokes the assumption that a Crusader cannot easily be a statesman; and that a monk cannot easily be a philosopher. Yet, to take only that special instance, it would be easy to point out that the cases of two famous men in the age of Frederick II would alone be strong enough to upset both the assumption and the antithesis. St. Louis, though a Crusader and even an unsuccessful Crusader, was really a far more successful statesman than Frederick II. By the test of practical politics, he popularised, solidified and sanctified the most powerful government in Europe, the order and concentration of the French Monarchy; the single dynasty that steadily increased its strength for five hundred years up to the glories of the Grand Siecle whereas Frederick went down in ruin before the Papacy and the Republics and a vast combination of priests and peoples. The Holy Roman Empire he wished to found was an ideal rather in the sense of a dream; it was certainly never a fact like the square and solid State which the French statesman did found. Or, to take another example from the next generation, one of the most strictly practical statesmen in history, our own Edward I, was also a Crusader.

The other half of the antithesis is even more false and here even more relevant. Frederick II was not a philosopher in the age of monks. He was a gentleman dabbling in philosophy in the age of the monk Thomas Aquinas. He was doubtless an intelligent and even brilliant gentleman; but if he did leave any notes on the nature of Being and Becoming, or the precise sense in which realities can be relative to Reality, I do not imagine those notes are now exciting undergraduates at Oxford or literary men in Paris, let alone the little groups of Thomists who have already sprung up even in New York and Chicago. It is no disrespect to the Emperor to say that he certainly was not a philosopher in the sense in which Thomas Aquinas was a philosopher, let alone so great or so universal or so permanent a philosopher. And Thomas Aquinas lived in that very age of monks, and in that very world of monks, which Macaulay talks of as if it were incapable of producing philosophy.

We need not dwell on the causes of this Victorian prejudice, which some still think so well advanced. It arose mainly from one narrow or insular notion; that no man could possibly be building up the best of the modern world, if he went with the main movement of the medieval world. These Victorians thought that only the heretic had ever helped humanity; only the man who nearly wrecked medieval civilisation could be of any use in constructing modern civilisation. Hence came a score of comic fables; as that the cathedrals must have been built by a secret society of Freemasons; or that the epic of Dante must be a cryptogram referring to the political hopes of Garibaldi. But the generalisation is not in its nature probable and it is not in fact true. This medieval period was rather specially the period of communal or corporate thinking, and in some matters it was really rather larger than the individualistic modern thinking. This could be proved in a flash from the mere fact of the use of the word 'statesman'. To a man of Macaulay's period, a statesman *always* meant a man who maintained the more narrow national interests of his own state against other states, as Richelieu maintained those of France, or Chatham of England, or Bismarck of Prussia. But if a man actually wanted to defend all these states, to combine all these states, to make a living brotherhood of all these states, to resist some outer peril as from the Mongolian millions—then that poor devil, of course, could not really be called a statesman. He was only a Crusader.

In this way it is but fair to Frederick II to say that he was a Crusader; if he was also rather like an Anti-Crusader. Certainly he was an international statesman. Indeed he was a particular type, which may be called an international soldier. The international soldier is always very much disliked by internationalists. They dislike Charlemagne and Charles V and Napoleon; and everybody who tried to create the World State for which they cry aloud day and night. But Frederick is more dubious and less doubted; he was supposed to be the head of the Holy Roman Empire; and accused of wanting to be the head of a very Unholy Roman Empire. But even if he were Antichrist, he would still be a witness to the unity of Christendom.

Nevertheless, there is a queer quality in that time; which, while it was international was also internal and intimate. War, in the wide modern sense, is possible, not because more men disagree, but because more men agree. Under the peculiarly modern coercions, such as Compulsory Education and Conscription, there are such very large *peaceful* areas, that they can all agree upon War. In that age men disagreed even about war; and peace might break out anywhere. Peace was interrupted by feuds and feuds by pardons. Individuality wound in and out of a maze; spiritual extremes were walled up with one another in one little walled town; and we see the great soul of Dante divided, a cloven flame; loving and hating his own city. This individual complexity is intensely vivid in the particular story we have here to tell, in a very rough outline. If anyone wishes to know what is meant by saying that action was more individual, and indeed incalculable, he may well note some of the stages in the story of the great feudal house of Aquino, which had its castle not far from Naples. In the mere hasty anecdote we have now to tell, we shall note in succession five or six stages of this sort. Landulf of Aquino, a heavy feudal fighter typical of the times, rode in armour behind the imperial banners, and attacked a monastery, because the Emperor regarded the monastery as a fortress held for his enemy the Pope. Later, we shall see the same feudal Lord sent his own son to the same monastery; probably on the friendly advice of the same Pope. Later still, another of his sons, entirely on his own, rebelled against the Emperor, and went over to the armies of the Pope. For this he was executed by the Emperor, with promptitude and despatch. I wish we knew more about that brother of Thomas Aquinas who risked and lost his life to support the cause of the Pope which was in all human essentials the cause of the People. He may not have been a saint; but he must have had some qualities of a martyr. Meanwhile, two other brothers, still ardent and active apparently in the service of the Emperor who killed the third brother, themselves proceeded to kidnap another brother, because they did not approve of his sympathy with the new social movements in religion. That is the sort of tangle in which this one distinguished medieval family found itself. It was not a war of nations, but it was a rather widespread family quarrel.

The reason for dwelling here, however, upon the position of the Emperor Frederick, as a type of his time, in his culture and his violence, in his concern for philosophy and his quarrel with religion, is not merely concerned with these things. He may here be the first figure that crosses the stage, because one of his very typical actions precipitated the first action, or obstinate inaction, which began the personal adventures of Thomas Aquinas in this world. The story also illustrates the extraordinary tangle in which a family like that of the Count of Aquino found itself; being at once so close to the Church and so much at odds with it. For Frederick II, in the course of these remarkable manoeuvres, military and political, which ranged from burning heretics to allying himself with Saracens, made a swoop as of a predatory eagle (and the Imperial eagle was rather predatory) upon a very large and wealthy monastery; the Benedictine Abbey of Monte Cassino; and stormed and sacked the place.

Some miles from the monastery of Monte Cassino stood a great crag or cliff, standing up like a pillar of the Apennines. It was crowned with a castle that bore the name of The Dry Rock, and was the eyrie in which the eaglets of the Aquino branch of the Imperial family were nursed to fly. Here lived Count Landulf of Aquino, who was the father of Thomas Aquinas and some seven other sons. In military affairs he doubtless rode with his family, in the feudal manner; and apparently had something to do with the destruction of the monastery. But it was typical of the tangle of the time, that Count Landulf seems afterwards to have thought that it would be a tactful and delicate act to put in his son Thomas as Abbot of the monastery. This would be of the nature of a graceful apology to the Church, and also, it would appear, the solution of a family difficulty.

For it had been long apparent to Count Landulf that nothing could be done with his seventh son Thomas, except to make him an Abbot or something of that kind. Born in 1226, he had from childhood a mysterious objection to becoming a predatory eagle, or even to taking an ordinary interest in falconry or tilting or any other gentlemanly pursuits. He was a large and heavy and quiet boy, and phenomenally silent, scarcely opening his mouth except to say suddenly to his schoolmaster in an explosive manner, "What is God?" The answer is not recorded but it is probable that the asker went on worrying out answers for himself. The only place for a person of this kind was the Church and presumably the cloister; and so far as that went, there was no particular difficulty. It was easy enough for a man in Count Landulf's position to arrange with some monastery for his son to be received there; and in this particular case he thought it would be a good idea if he were received in some official capacity, that would be worthy of his worldly rank. So everything was smoothly arranged for Thomas Aquinas becoming a monk, which would seem to be what he himself wanted; and sooner or later becoming Abbot of Monte Cassino. And then the curious thing happened.

In so far as we may follow rather dim and disputed events, it would seem that the young Thomas Aquinas walked into his father's castle one day and calmly announced that he had become one of the Begging Friars, of the new order founded by Dominic the Spaniard; much as the eldest son of the squire might go home and airily inform the family that he had married a gypsy; or the heir of a Tory Duke state that he was walking tomorrow with the Hunger Marchers organised by alleged Communists. By this, as has been noted already, we may pretty well measure the abyss between the old monasticism and the new, and the earthquake of the Dominican and Franciscan revolution. Thomas had appeared to wish to be a Monk; and the gates were silently opened to him and the long avenues of the abbey, the very carpet, so to speak, laid for him up to the throne of the mitred abbot. He said he wished to be a Friar, and his family flew at him like wild beasts; his brothers pursued him along the public roads, half-rent his friar's frock from his back and finally locked him up in a tower like a lunatic.

It is not very easy to trace the course of this furious family quarrel, and how it eventually spent itself against the tenacity of the young Friar; according to some stories, his mother's disapproval was short-lived and she went over to his side; but it was not only his relatives that were embroiled. We might say that the central governing class of Europe, which partly consisted of his family, were in a turmoil over the deplorable youth; even the Pope was asked for tactful intervention, and it was at one time proposed that Thomas should be allowed to wear the Dominican habit while acting as Abbot in the Benedictine Abbey. To many this would seem a tactful compromise; but it did not commend itself to the narrow medieval mind of Thomas Aquinas. He indicated sharply that he wished to be a Dominican in the Dominican Order, and not at a fancy-dress ball; and the diplomatic proposal appears to have been dropped.

Thomas of Aquino wanted to be a Friar. It was a staggering fact to his contemporaries; and it is rather an intriguing fact even to us; for this desire, limited literally and strictly to this statement, was the one practical thing to which his will was clamped with adamantine obstinacy till his death. He would not be an Abbot; he would not be a Monk; he would not even be a Prior or ruler in his own fraternity; he would not be a prominent or important Friar; he would be a Friar. It is as if Napoleon had insisted on remaining a private soldier all his life. Something in this heavy, quiet, cultivated, rather academic gentleman would not be satisfied till he was, by fixed authoritative proclamation and official pronouncement, established and appointed to be a Beggar. It is all the more interesting because, while he did more than his duty a thousand times over, he was not at all like a Beggar; nor at all likely to be a good Beggar. He had nothing of the native vagabond about him, as had his great precursors; he was not born with something of the wandering minstrel, like St. Francis; or something of the tramping missionary, like St. Dominic. But he insisted upon putting himself under military orders, to do these things at the will of another, if required. He may be compared with some of the more magnanimous aristocrats who have enrolled themselves in revolutionary armies; or some of the best of the poets and scholars who volunteered as private soldiers in the Great War. Something in the courage and consistency of Dominic and Francis had challenged his deep sense of justice; and while remaining a very reasonable person, and even a diplomatic one, he never let anything shake the iron immobility of this one decision of his youth; nor was he to be turned from his tall and towering ambition to take the lowest place.

The first effect of his decision, as we have seen, was much more stimulating and even startling. The General of the Dominicans, under whom Thomas had enrolled himself, was probably well aware of the diplomatic attempts to dislodge him and the worldly difficulties of resisting them. His expedient was to take his young follower out of Italy altogether; bidding him proceed with a few other friars to Paris. There was something prophetic even about this first progress of the travelling teacher of the nations; for Paris was indeed destined to be in some sense the goal of his spiritual journey; since it was there that he was to deliver both his great defence of the Friars and his great defiance to the antagonists of Aristotle. But this his first journey to Paris was destined to be broken off very short indeed. The friars had reached a turn of the road by a wayside fountain, a little way north of Rome, when they were overtaken by a wild cavalcade of captors, who seized on Thomas like brigands, but who were in fact only rather needlessly agitated brothers. He had a large number of brothers: perhaps only two were here involved. Indeed he was the seventh; and friends of Birth Control may lament that this philosopher was needlessly added to the noble line of ruffians who kidnapped him. It was an odd affair altogether. There is something quaint and picturesque in the idea of kidnapping a begging friar, who might in a sense be called a runaway abbot. There is a comic and tragic tangle in the motives and purposes of such a trio of strange kinsmen. There is a sort of Christian cross-purposes in the contrast between the feverish illusion of the importance of things, always marking men who are called practical; and the much more practical pertinacity of the man who is called theoretical.

Thus at least did those three strange brethren stagger or trail along their tragic road, tied together, as it were, like criminal and constable; only that the criminals were making the arrest. So their figures are seen for an instant against the horizon of history; brothers as sinister as any since Cain and Abel. For this queer outrage in the great family of Aquino does really stand out symbolically, as representing something that will forever make the Middle Ages a mystery and a bewilderment; capable of sharply contrasted interpretations like darkness and light. For in two of those men there raged, we might say screamed, a savage pride of blood and blazonry of arms, though they were princes of the most refined world of their time, which would seem more suitable to a tribe dancing round a totem. For the moment they had forgotten everything except the name of a family, that is narrower than a tribe, and far narrower than a nation. And the third figure of that trio, born of the same mother and perhaps visibly one with the others in face or form, had a conception of brotherhood broader than most modern democracy, for it was not national but international; a faith in mercy and modesty far deeper than any mere mildness of manners in the modern world; and a drastic oath of poverty, which would now be counted quite a mad exaggeration of the revolt against plutocracy and pride. Out of the same Italian castle came two savages and one sage; or one saint more pacific than most modern sages. That is the double aspect confusing a hundred controversies. That is what makes the riddle of the medieval age; that it was not one age but two ages. We look into the moods of some men, and it might be the Stone Age; we look into the minds of other men, and they might be living in the Golden Age; in the most modern sort of Utopia. There were always good men and bad men; but in this time good men who were subtle lived with bad men who were simple. They lived in the same family; they were brought up in the same nursery; and they came out to struggle, as the brothers of Aquino struggled by the wayside, when they dragged the new friar along the road and shut him up in the castle on the hill.

When his relations tried to despoil him of his friar's frock he seems to have laid about them in the fighting manner of his fathers, and it would seem successfully, since this attempt was abandoned. He accepted the imprisonment itself with his customary composure, and probably did not mind very much whether he was left to philosophise in a dungeon or in a cell. Indeed there is something in the way the whole tale is told, which suggests that through a great part of that strange abduction, he had been carried about like a lumbering stone statue. Only one tale told of his captivity shows him merely in anger; and that shows him angrier than he ever was before or after. It struck the imagination of his own time for more important reasons; but it has an interest that is psychological as well as moral. For once in his life, for the first time and the last, Thomas of Aquino was really *hors de lui*; riding a storm outside that tower of intellect and contemplation in which he commonly lived. And that was when his brothers introduced into his room some specially gorgeous and painted courtesan, with the idea of surprising him by a sudden temptation, or at least involving him in a scandal. His anger was justified, even by less strict moral standards than his own; for the meanness was even worse than the foulness of the expedient. Even on the lowest grounds, he knew his brothers knew, and they knew that he knew, that it was an insult to him as a gentleman to suppose that he would break his pledge upon so base a provocation; and he had behind him a far more terrible sensibility; all that huge ambition of humility which was to him the voice of God out of heaven. In this one flash alone we see that huge unwieldy figure in an attitude of activity, or even animation; and he was very animated indeed. He sprang from his seat and snatched a brand out of the fire, and stood brandishing it like a flaming sword. The woman not unnaturally shrieked and fled, which was all that he wanted; but it is quaint to think of what she must have thought of that madman of monstrous stature juggling with flames and apparently threatening to burn down the house. All he did, however, was to stride after her to the door and bang and bar it behind her; and then, with a sort of impulse of violent ritual, he rammed the burning brand into the door, blackening and blistering it with one big black sign of the cross. Then he returned, and dropped it again into the fire; and sat down on that seat of sedentary scholarship, that chair of philosophy, that secret throne of contemplation, from which he never rose again.

CHAPTER III

THE ARISTOTELIAN REVOLUTION

Albert, the Swabian, rightly called the Great, was the founder of modern science. He did more than any other man to prepare that process, which has turned the alchemist into the chemist, and the astrologer into the astronomer. It is odd that, having been in his time, in this sense almost the first astronomer, he now lingers in legend almost as the last astrologer. Serious historians are abandoning the absurd notion that the mediaeval Church persecuted all scientists as wizards. It is very nearly the opposite of the truth. The world sometimes persecuted them as wizards, and sometimes ran after them as wizards; the sort of pursuing that is the reverse of persecuting. The Church alone regarded them really and solely as scientists. Many an enquiring cleric was charged with mere magic in making his lenses and mirrors; he was charged by his rude and rustic neighbours; and would probably have been charged in exactly the same way if they had been Pagan neighbours or Puritan neighbours or Seventh-Day Adventist neighbours. But even then he stood a better chance when judged by the Papacy, than if he had been merely lynched by the laity. The Catholic Pontiff did not denounce Albertus Magnus as a magician. It was the half-heathen tribes of the north who admired him as a magician. It is the half-heathen tribes of the industrial towns today, the readers of cheap dream-books, and quack pamphlets, and newspaper prophets, who still admire him as an astrologer. It is admitted that the range of his recorded knowledge, of strictly material and mechanical facts, was amazing in a man of his time. It is true that, in most other cases, there was a certain limitation to the data of medieval science; but this certainly had nothing to do with medieval religion. For the data of Aristotle, and the great Greek civilisation, were in many ways more limited still. But it is not really so much a question of access to the facts, as of attitude to the facts. Most of the Schoolmen, if informed by the only informants they had that a unicorn has one horn or a salamander lives in the fire, still used it more as an illustration of logic than an incident of life. What they really said was, "If a Unicorn has one horn, two unicorns have as many horns as one cow." And that has not one inch the less a fact because the unicorn is a fable. But with Albertus in medieval times, as with Aristotle in ancient times, there did begin something like the idea of emphasising the question: "But does the unicorn only have one horn or the salamander a fire instead of a fireside?" Doubtless when the social and geographical limits of medieval life began to allow them to search the fire for salamanders or the desert for unicorns, they had to modify many of their scientific ideas. A fact which will expose them to the very proper scorn of a generation of scientists which has just discovered that Newton is nonsense, that space is limited, and that there is no such thing as an atom.

This great German, known in his most famous period as a professor in Paris, was previously for some time professor at Cologne. In that beautiful Roman city, there gathered round him in thousands the lovers of that extraordinary life; the student life of the Middle Ages. They came together in great groups called Nations; and the fact illustrates very well the difference between medieval nationalism and modern nationalism. For although there might any morning be a brawl between the Spanish students and the Scottish students, or between the Flemish and the French, and swords flash or stones fly on the most purely patriotic principles, the fact remains that they had all come to the same school to learn the same philosophy. And though that might not prevent the starting of a quarrel, it might have a great deal to do with the ending of it. Before these motley groups of men from the ends of the earth, the father of science unrolled his scroll of strange wisdom; of sun and comet, of fish and bird. He was an Aristotelian developing, as it were, the one experimental hint of Aristotle; and in this he was entirely original. He cared less to be original about the deeper matters of men and morals; about which he was content to hand on a decent and Christianised Aristotelianism; he was even in a sense ready to compromise upon the merely metaphysical issue of the Nominalists and the Realists. He would never have maintained alone the great war that was coming, for a balanced and humanised Christianity; but when it came, he was entirely on its side. He was called the Universal Doctor, because of the range of his scientific studies; yet he was in truth a specialist. The popular legend is never quite wrong; if a man of science is a magician, he was a magician. And the man of science has always been much *more* of a magician than the priest; since he would "control the elements" rather than submit to the Spirit who is more elementary than the elements.

Among the students thronging into the lecture-rooms there was one student, conspicuous by his tall and bulky figure, and completely failing or refusing to be conspicuous for anything else. He was so dumb in the debates that his fellows began to assume an American significance in the word dumbness; for in that land it is a synonym for dullness. It is clear that, before long, even his imposing stature began to have only the ignominious immensity of the big boy left behind in the lowest form. He was called the Dumb Ox. He was the object, not merely of mockery, but of pity. One good-natured student pitied him so much as to try to help him with his lessons, going over the elements of logic like an alphabet in a horn-book. The dunce thanked him with pathetic politeness; and the philanthropist went on swimmingly, till he came to a passage about which he was himself a little doubtful; about which, in point of fact, he was wrong. Whereupon the dunce, with every appearance of embarrassment and disturbance, pointed out a possible solution which happened to be right. The benevolent student was left staring, as at a monster, at this mysterious lump of ignorance and intelligence; and strange whispers began to run round the schools.

A regular religious biographer of Thomas Aquinas (who, needless to say, was the dunce in question) has said that by the end of this interview "his love of truth overcame his humility;" which, properly understood, is precisely true. But it does not, in the secondary psychological and social sense, describe all the welter of elements that went on within that massive head. All the relatively few anecdotes about Aquinas have a very peculiar vividness if we visualise the type of man; and this is an excellent example. Amid those elements was something of the difficulty which the generalising intellect has in adapting itself suddenly to a tiny detail of daily life; there was something of the shyness of really well-bred people about showing off; there was something even, perhaps, of that queer paralysis, and temptation to prefer even misunderstandings to long explanations, which led Sir James Barrie, in his amusing sketch, to allow himself to be saddled with a Brother Henry he never possessed, rather than exert himself to put in a word of warning. These other elements doubtless worked with the very extraordinary humility of this very extraordinary man; but another element worked with his equally unquestionable "love of truth" in bringing the misunderstanding to an end. It is an element that must never be left out of the make-up of St. Thomas. However dreamy or distracted or immersed in theories he might be, he had any amount of Common Sense; and by the time it came, not only to being taught, but to being taught wrong, there was something in him that said sharply, "Oh, this has got to stop!"

It seems probable that it was Albertus Magnus himself, the lecturer and learned teacher of all these youths, who first suspected something of the kind. He gave Thomas small jobs to do, of annotation or exposition; he persuaded him to banish his bashfulness so as to take part in at least one debate. He was a very shrewd old man and had studied the habits of other animals besides the salamander and the unicorn. He had studied many specimens of the most monstrous of all monstrosities; that is called Man. He knew the signs and marks of the sort of man, who is in an innocent way something of a monster among men. He was too good a schoolmaster not to know that the dunce is not always a dunce. He learned with amusement that this dunce had been nicknamed the Dumb Ox by his school-fellows. All that is natural enough; but it does not take away the savour of something rather strange and symbolic, about the extraordinary emphasis with which he spoke at last. For Aquinas was still generally known only as one obscure and obstinately unresponsive pupil, among many more brilliant and promising pupils, when the great Albert broke silence with his famous cry and prophecy; "You call him a Dumb Ox: I tell you this Dumb Ox shall bellow so loud that his bellowings will fill the world."

To Albertus Magnus, as to Aristotle or Augustine or any number of other and older teachers, St. Thomas was always ready, with the hearty sort of humility, to give thanks for all his thinking. None the less, his own thinking was an advance on Albertus and the other Aristotelians, just as it was an advance on Augustine and the Augustinians. Albert had drawn attention to the direct study of natural facts, if only through fables like the unicorn and the salamander but the monster called Man awaited a much more subtle and flexible vivisection. The two men, however, became close friends and their friendship counts for a great deal in this central fight of the Middle Ages. For, as we shall see, the rehabilitation of Aristotle was a revolution almost as revolutionary as the exaltation of Dominic and Francis; and St. Thomas was destined to play a striking part in both.

It will be realised that the Aquino family had ultimately abandoned its avenging pursuit of its ugly duckling; who, as a black friar, should perhaps be called its black sheep. Of that escape some picturesque stories are told. The black sheep generally profits at last by quarrels among the white sheep of a family. They begin by quarrelling with him, but they end by quarrelling with each other. There is a rather confusing account concerning which members of his family came over to his side, while he was still imprisoned in the tower. But it is a fact that he was very fond of his sisters, and therefore probably not a fable that it was they who engineered his escape. According to the story, they rigged up a rope to the top of the tower, attached to a big basket, and it must have been rather a big basket if he was indeed lowered in this fashion from his prison, and escaped into the world. Anyhow, he did escape by energy, external or internal. But it was only an individual energy. The world was still pursuing and persecuting the Friars, quite as much as when they fled along the road to Rome. Thomas Aquinas had the good fortune to gather under the shadow of the one great outstanding Friar, whose respectability it was difficult to dispute, the learned and orthodox Albertus; but even he and his were soon troubled by the growing storm that threatened the new popular movements in the Church. Albertus was summoned to Paris, to receive the degree of a Doctor; but everyone knew that every move in that game had the character of a challenge. He made only the request, which probably looked like an eccentric request, that he should take his Dumb Ox with him. They set out, like ordinary Friars or religious vagabonds; they slept in such monasteries as they could find; and finally in the monastery of St. James in Paris, where Thomas met another Friar who was also another friend.

Perhaps under the shadow of the storm that menaced all Friars, Bonaventure, the Franciscan, grew into so great a friendship with Thomas the Dominican, that their contemporaries compared them to David and Jonathan. The point is of some interest; because it would be quite easy to represent the Franciscan and the Dominican as flatly contradicting each other. The Franciscan may be represented as the Father of all the Mystics; and the Mystics can be represented as men who maintain that the final fruition or joy of the soul is rather a sensation than a thought. The motto of the Mystics has always been, "Taste and see." Now St. Thomas also began by saying, "Taste and see;" but he said it of the first rudimentary impressions of the human animal. It might well be maintained that the Franciscan puts Taste last and the Dominican puts it first. It might be said that the Thomist begins with something solid like the taste of an apple, and afterwards deduces a divine life for the intellect; while the Mystic exhausts the intellect first, and says finally that the sense of God is something like the taste of an apple. A common enemy might claim that St. Thomas begins with the taste of fruit and St. Bonaventure ends with the taste of fruit. But they are both right; if I may say so, it is a privilege of people who contradict each other in their cosmos to be both right. The Mystic is right in saying that the relation of God and Man is essentially a love-story; the pattern and type of all love-stories. The Dominican rationalist is equally right in saying that the intellect is at home in the topmost heavens; and that the appetite for truth may outlast and even devour all the duller appetites of man.

At the moment Aquinas and Bonaventure were encouraged in the possibility that they were both right; by the almost universal agreement that they were both wrong. It was in any case a time of wild disturbance, and, as is common in such times, those who were trying to put things right were most vigorously accused of putting things wrong. Nobody knew who would win in that welter: Islam, or the Manichees of the Midi; or the two-faced and mocking Emperor; or the Crusades; or the old Orders of Christendom. But some men had a very vivid feeling that everything was breaking up; and that all the recent experiments or excesses were part of the same social dissolution; and there were two things that such men regarded as signs of ruin; one was the awful apparition of Aristotle out of the East, a sort of Greek god supported by Arabian worshippers; and the other was the new freedom of the Friars. It was the opening of the monastery and the scattering of the monks to wander over the world. The general feeling that they wandered like sparks from a furnace hitherto contained; the furnace of the abnormal love of God: the sense that they would utterly unbalance the common people with the counsels of perfection; that they would drift into being demagogues; all this finally burst out in a famous book called *The Perils of the Latter Times*, by a furious reactionary, William de St. Amour. It challenged the French King and the Pope, so that they established an enquiry. And Aquinas and Bonaventure, the two incongruous friends, with their respectively topsy-turvy universes, went up to Rome together, to defend the freedom of the Friars.

Thomas Aquinas defended the great vow of his youth, for freedom and for the poor; and it was probably the topmost moment of his generally triumphant career; for he turned back the whole backward movement of his time. Responsible authorities have said that, but for him, the whole great popular movement of the Friars might have been destroyed. With this popular victory the shy and awkward student finally becomes a historical character and a public man. After that, he was identified with the Mendicant Orders. But while St. Thomas may be said to have made his name in the defence of the Mendicant Orders against the reactionaries, who took the same view of them as his own family had taken, there is generally a difference between a man making his name and a man really doing his work. The work of Thomas Aquinas was yet to come; but less shrewd observers than he could already see that it was coming. Broadly speaking, the danger was the danger of the orthodox, or those who too easily identify the old order with the orthodox, forcing a final and conclusive condemnation of Aristotle. There had already been rash and random condemnations to that effect, issued here and there, and the pressure of the narrower Augustinians upon the Pope and the principal judges became daily more pressing. The peril had appeared, not unnaturally, because of the historical and geographical accident of the Moslem proximity to the culture of Byzantium. The Arabs had got hold of the Greek manuscripts before the Latins who were the true heirs of the Greeks. And Moslems, though not very orthodox Moslems, were turning Aristotle into a pantheist philosophy still less acceptable to orthodox Christians. This second controversy, however, requires more explanation than the first. As is remarked on an introductory page, most modern people do know that St. Francis at least was a liberator of large sympathies; that, whatever their positive view of medievalism, the Friars were in a relative sense a popular movement, pointing to greater fraternity and freedom; and a very little further information would inform them that this was every bit as true of the Dominican as of the Franciscan Friars. Nobody now is particularly likely to start up in defence of feudal abbots or fixed and stationary monks, against such impudent innovators as St. Francis and St. Thomas. We may therefore be allowed to summarise briefly the great debate about the Friars, though it shook all Christendom in its day. But the greater debate about Aristotle presents a greater difficulty; because there are modern misconceptions about it which can only be approached with a little more elaboration.

Perhaps there is really no such thing as a Revolution recorded in history. What happened was always a Counter-Revolution. Men were always rebelling against the last rebels; or even repenting of the last rebellion. This could be seen in the most casual contemporary fashions, if the fashionable mind had not fallen into the habit of seeing the very latest rebel as rebelling against all ages at once. The Modern Girl with the lipstick and the cocktail is as much a rebel against the Woman's Rights Woman of the '80's, with her stiff stick-up collars and strict teetotalism, as the latter was a rebel against the Early Victorian lady of the languid waltz tunes and the album full of quotations from Byron: or as the last, again, was a rebel against a Puritan mother to whom the waltz was a wild orgy and Byron the Bolshevist of his age. Trace even the Puritan mother back through history and she represents a rebellion against the Cavalier laxity of the English Church, which was at first a rebel against the Catholic civilisation, which had been a rebel against the Pagan civilisation. Nobody but a lunatic could pretend that these things were a progress; for they obviously go first one way and then the other. But whichever is right, one thing is certainly wrong; and that is the modern habit of looking at them only from the modern end. For that is only to see the end of the tale; they rebel against they know not what, because it arose they know not when; intent only on its ending, they are ignorant of its beginning; and therefore of its very being. The difference between the smaller cases and the larger, is that in the latter there is really so huge a human upheaval that men start from it like men in a new world; and that very novelty enables them to go on very long; and generally to go on too long. It is *because* these things start with a vigorous revolt that the intellectual impetus lasts long enough to make them seem like a survival. An excellent example of this is the real story of the revival and the neglect of Aristotle. By the end of the medieval time, Aristotelianism did eventually grow stale. Only a very fresh and successful novelty ever gets quite so stale as that.

When the moderns, drawing the blackest curtain of obscurantism that ever obscured history, decided that nothing mattered much before the Renaissance and the Reformation, they instantly began their modern career by falling into a big blunder. It was the blunder about Platonism. They found, hanging about the courts of the swaggering princes of the sixteenth century (which was as far back in history as they were allowed to go) certain anti-clerical artists and scholars who said they were bored with Aristotle and were supposed to be secretly indulging in Plato. The moderns, utterly ignorant of the whole story of the medievals, instantly fell into the trap. They assumed that Aristotle was some crabbed antiquity and tyranny from the black back of the Dark Ages, and that Plato was an entirely new Pagan pleasure never yet tasted by Christian men. Father Knox has shown in what a startling state of innocence is the mind of Mr. H. L. Mencken, for instance, upon this point. In fact, of course, the story is exactly the other way round. If anything, it was Platonism that was the old orthodoxy. It was Aristotelianism that was the very modern revolution. And the leader of that modern revolution was the man who is the subject of this book.

The truth is that the historical Catholic Church began by being Platonist; by being rather too Platonist. Platonism was in that golden Greek air that was breathed by the first great Greek theologians. The Christian Fathers were much more like the Neo-Platonists than were the scholars of the Renaissance; who were only Neo-Neo-Platonists. For Chrysostom or Basil it was as ordinary and normal to think in terms of the Logos, or the Wisdom which is the aim of philosophers, as it is to any men of any religion today to talk about social problems or progress or the economic crisis throughout the world. St. Augustine followed a natural mental evolution when he was a Platonist before he was a Manichean, and a Manichean before he was a Christian. And it was exactly in that last association that the first faint hint, of the danger of being *too* Platonist, may be seen.

From the Renaissance to the nineteenth century, the Moderns have had an almost monstrous love of the Ancients. In considering medieval life, they could never regard the Christians as anything but the pupils of the Pagans; of Plato in ideas, or Aristotle in reason and science. It was not so. On some points, even from the most monotonously modern standpoint, Catholicism was centuries ahead of Platonism or Aristotelianism. We can see it still, for instance, in the tiresome tenacity of Astrology. On that matter the philosophers were all in favour of superstition; and the saints and all such superstitious people were against superstition. But even the great saints found it difficult to get disentangled from this superstition. Two points were always put by those suspicious of the Aristotelianism of Aquinas; and they sound to us now very quaint and comic, taken together. One was the view that the stars are personal beings, governing our lives: the other the great general theory that men have one mind between them; a view obviously opposed to immortality; that is, to individuality. Both linger among the Moderns: so strong is still the tyranny of the Ancients. Astrology sprawls over the Sunday papers, and the other doctrine has its hundredth form in what is called Communism: or the Soul of the Hive.

For on one preliminary point, this position must not be misunderstood. When we praise the practical value of the Aristotelian Revolution, and the originality of Aquinas in leading it, we do not mean that the Scholastic philosophers before him had not been philosophers, or had not been highly philosophical, or had not been in touch with ancient philosophy. In so far as there was ever a bad break in philosophical history, it was not before St. Thomas, or at the beginning of medieval history; it was after St. Thomas and at the beginning of modern history. The great intellectual tradition that comes down to us from Pythagoras and Plato was never interrupted or lost through such trifles as the sack of Rome, the triumph of Attila or all the barbarian invasions of the Dark Ages. It was only lost after the introduction of printing, the discovery of America, the founding of the Royal Society and all the enlightenment of the Renaissance and the modern world. It was there, if anywhere, that there was lost or impatiently snapped the long thin delicate thread that had descended from distant antiquity; the thread of that unusual human hobby; the habit of thinking. This is proved by the fact that the printed books of this later period largely had to wait for the eighteenth century, or the end of the seventeenth century, to find even the names of the new philosophers;

who were at the best a new kind of philosophers. But the decline of the Empire, the Dark Ages and the early Middle Ages, though too much tempted to neglect what was opposed to Platonic philosophy, had never neglected philosophy. In that sense St. Thomas, like most other very original men, has a long and clear pedigree. He himself is constantly referring back to the authorities from St. Augustine to St. Anselm, and from St. Anselm to St. Albert, and even when he differs, he also defers.

A very learned Anglican once said to me, not perhaps without a touch of tartness, "I can't understand why everybody talks as if Thomas Aquinas were the beginning of the Scholastic philosophy. I could understand their saying he was the end of it." Whether or no the comment was meant to be tart, we may be sure that the reply of St. Thomas would have been perfectly urbane. And indeed it would be easy to answer with a certain placidity, that in his Thomist language the end of a thing does not mean its destruction, but its fulfilment. No Thomist will complain, if Thomism is the end of our philosophy, in the sense in which God is the end of our existence. For that does not mean that we cease to exist, but that we become as perennial as the *philosophia perennis*. Putting this claim on one side, however, it is important to remember that my distinguished interlocutor was perfectly right, in that there had been whole dynasties of doctrinal philosophers before Aquinas, leading up to the day of the great revolt of the Aristotelians. Nor was even that revolt a thing entirely abrupt and unforeseen. An able writer in the *Dublin Review* not long ago pointed out that in some respects the whole nature of metaphysics had advanced a long way since Aristotle, by the time it came to Aquinas. And that it is no disrespect to the primitive and gigantic genius of the Stagirite to say that in some respects he was really but a rude and rough founder of philosophy, compared with some of the subsequent subtleties of medievalism; that the Greek gave a few grand hints which the Scholastics developed into the most delicate fine shades. This may be an overstatement, but there is a truth in it. Anyhow, it is certain that even in Aristotelian philosophy, let alone Platonic philosophy, there was already a tradition of highly intelligent interpretation. If that delicacy afterwards degenerated into hair-splitting, it was none the less delicate hair-splitting; and work requiring very scientific tools.

What made the Aristotelian Revolution really revolutionary was the fact that it was really religious. It is the fact, so fundamental that I thought it well to lay it down in the first few pages of this book; that the revolt was largely a revolt of the most Christian elements in Christendom. St. Thomas, every bit as much as St. Francis, felt subconsciously that the hold of his people was slipping on the solid Catholic doctrine and discipline, worn smooth by more than a thousand years of routine; and that the Faith needed to be shown under a new light and dealt with from another angle. But he had no motive except the desire to make it popular for the salvation of the people. It was true, broadly speaking, that for some time past it had been too Platonist to be popular. It needed something like the shrewd and homely touch of Aristotle to turn it again into a religion of common sense. Both the motive and the method are illustrated in the war of Aquinas against the Augustinians.

First, it must be remembered that the Greek influence continued to flow from the Greek Empire; or at least from the centre of the Roman Empire which was in the Greek city of Byzantium, and no longer in Rome. That influence was Byzantine in every good and bad sense; like Byzantine art, it was severe and mathematical and a little terrible; like Byzantine etiquette, it was Oriental and faintly decadent. We owe to the learning of Mr. Christopher Dawson much enlightenment upon the way in which Byzantium slowly stiffened into a sort of Asiatic theocracy, more like that which served the Sacred Emperor in China. But even the unlearned can see the difference, in the way in which Eastern Christianity flattened everything, as it flattened the faces of the images into icons. It became a thing of patterns rather than pictures; and it made definite and destructive war upon statues. Thus we see, strangely enough, that the East was the land of the Cross and the West was the land of the Crucifix. The Greeks were being dehumanised by a radiant symbol, while the Goths were being humanised by an instrument of torture. Only the West made realistic pictures of the greatest of all the tales out of the East. Hence the Greek element in Christian theology tended more and more to be a sort of dried up Platonism; a thing of diagrams and abstractions; to the last indeed noble abstractions, but not sufficiently touched by that great thing that is by definition almost the opposite of abstraction: Incarnation. Their Logos was the Word; but not the Word made Flesh. In a thousand very subtle ways, often escaping doctrinal definition, this spirit spread over the world of Christendom from the place where the Sacred Emperor sat under his golden mosaics; and the flat pavement of the Roman Empire was at last a sort of smooth pathway for Mahomet. For Islam was the ultimate fulfilment of the Iconoclasts. Long before that, however, there was this tendency to make the Cross merely decorative like the Crescent; to make it a pattern like the Greek key or the Wheel of Buddha. But there is something passive about such a world of patterns, and the Greek Key does not open any door, while the Wheel of Buddha always moves round and never moves on.

Partly through these negative influences, partly through a necessary and noble asceticism which sought to emulate the awful standard of the martyrs, the earlier Christian ages had been excessively anti-corporeal and too near the danger-line of Manichean mysticism. But there was far less danger in the fact that the saints macerated the body than in the fact that the sages neglected it. Granted all the grandeur of Augustine's contribution to Christianity, there was in a sense a more subtle danger in Augustine the Platonist than even in Augustine the Manichee. There came from it a mood which unconsciously committed the heresy of dividing the substance of the Trinity. It thought of God too exclusively as a Spirit who purifies or a Saviour who redeems; and too little as a Creator who creates. That is why men like Aquinas thought it right to correct Plato by an appeal to Aristotle; Aristotle who took things as he found them, just as Aquinas accepted things as God created them. In all the work of St. Thomas the world of positive creation is perpetually present. Humanly speaking, it was he who saved the human element in Christian theology, if he used for convenience certain elements in heathen philosophy. Only, as has already been urged, the human element is also the Christian one.

The panic upon the Aristotelian peril, that had passed across the high places of the Church, was probably a dry wind from the desert. It was really filled rather with fear of Mahomet than fear of Aristotle. And this was ironic, because there was really much more difficulty in reconciling Aristotle with Mahomet than in reconciling him with Christ. Islam is essentially a simple creed for simple men; and nobody can ever really turn pantheism into a simple creed. It is at once too abstract and too complicated. There are simple believers in a personal God; and there are atheists more simple-minded than any believers in a personal God. But few can, in mere simplicity, accept a godless universe as a god. And while the Moslem, as compared with the Christian, had perhaps a less human God, he had if possible a more personal God. The will of Allah was very much of a will, and could not be turned into a stream of tendency. On all that cosmic and abstract side the Catholic was more accommodating than the Moslem—up to a point. The Catholic could admit at least that Aristotle was right about the impersonal elements of a personal God. Hence, we may say broadly of the Moslem philosophers, that those who became good philosophers became bad Moslems. It is not altogether unnatural that many bishops and doctors feared that the Thomists might become good philosophers and bad Christians. But there were also many, of the strict school of Plato and Augustine, who stoutly denied that they were even good philosophers. Between those rather incongruous passions, the love of Plato and the fear of Mahomet, there was a moment when the prospects of any Aristotelian culture in Christendom looked very dark indeed. Anathema after anathema was thundered from high places; and under the shadow of the persecution, as so often happens, it seemed for a moment that barely one or two figures stood alone in the storm-swept area. They were both in the black and white of the Dominicans; for Albertus and Aquinas stood firm.

In that sort of combat there is always confusion; and majorities change into minorities and back again, as if by magic. It is always difficult to date the turn of the tide, which seems to be a welter of eddies; the very dates seeming to overlap and confuse the crisis. But the change, from the moment when the two Dominicans stood alone to the moment when the whole Church at last wheeled into line with them, may perhaps be found at about the moment when they were practically brought before a hostile but a not unjust judge. Stephen Tempier, the Bishop of Paris, was apparently a rather fine specimen of the old fanatical Churchman, who thought that admiring Aristotle was a weakness likely to be followed by adoring Apollo. He was also, by a piece of bad luck, one of the old social conservatives, who had intensely resented the popular revolution of the Preaching Friars. But he was an honest man; and Thomas Aquinas never asked for anything but permission to address honest men. All around him there were other Aristotelian revolutionaries of a much more dubious sort. There was Siger, the sophist from Brabant, who learned all his Aristotelianism from the Arabs; and had an ingenious theory about how an Arabian agnostic could also be a Christian. There were a thousand young men of the sort that had shouted for Abelard; full of the youth of the thirteenth century and drunken with the Greek wine of Stagira. Over against them, lowering and implacable, was the old Puritan party of the Augustinians; only too delighted to class the rationalistic Albert and Thomas with equivocal Moslem meta-physicians.

It would seem that the triumph of Thomas was really a personal triumph. He withdrew not a single one of his propositions; though it is said that the reactionary Bishop did condemn some of them after his death. On the whole, however, Aquinas convinced most of his critics that he was quite as good a Catholic as they were. There was a sequel of squabbles between the Religious Orders, following upon this controversial crisis. But it is probably true to say that the fact, that a man like Aquinas had managed even partially to satisfy a man like Tempier, was the end of the essential quarrel. What was already familiar to the few became familiar to the many; that an Aristotelian could really be a Christian. Another fact assisted in the common conversion. It rather curiously resembles the story of the translation of the Bible; and the alleged Catholic suppression of the Bible. Behind the scenes, where the Pope was much more tolerant than the Paris Bishop, the friends of Aquinas had been hard at work producing a new translation of Aristotle. It demonstrated that in many ways the heretical translation had been a very herctical translation. With the final consummation of this work, we may say that the great Greek philosophy entered finally into the system of Christendom. The process has been half humourously described as the Baptism of Aristotle.

We have all heard of the humility of the man of science; of many who were very genuinely humble; and of some who were very proud of their humility. It will be the somewhat too recurrent burden of this brief study that Thomas Aquinas really did have the humility of the man of science; as a special variant of the humility of the saint. It is true that he did not himself contribute anything concrete in the experiment or detail of physical science; in this, it may be said, he even lagged behind the last generation, and was far less of an experimental scientist than his tutor Albertus Magnus. But for all that, he was historically a great friend to the freedom of science. The principles he laid down, properly understood, are perhaps the best that can be produced for protecting science from mere obscurantist persecution. For instance, in the matter of the inspiration of Scripture, he fixed first on the obvious fact, which was forgotten by four furious centuries of sectarian battle, that the meaning of Scripture is very far from self-evident and that we must often interpret it in the light of other truths. If a literal interpretation is really and flatly contradicted by an obvious fact, why then we can only say that the literal interpretation must be a false interpretation. But the fact must really be an obvious fact. And unfortunately, nineteenth century scientists were just as ready to jump to the conclusion that any guess about nature was an obvious fact, as were seventeenth-century sectarians to jump to the conclusion that any guess about Scripture was the obvious explanation. Thus, private theories about what the Bible ought to mean, and premature theories about what the world ought to mean, have met in loud and widely advertised controversy, especially in the Victorian time; and this clumsy collision of two very impatient forms of ignorance was known as the quarrel of Science and Religion.

But St. Thomas had the scientific humility in this very vivid and special sense; that he was ready to take the lowest place; for the examination of the lowest things. He did not, like a modern specialist, study the worm as if it were the world; but he was willing to begin to study the reality of the world in the reality of the worm. His Aristotelianism simply meant that the study of the humblest fact will lead to the study of the highest truth. That for him the process was logical and not biological, was concerned with philosophy rather than science, does not alter the essential idea that he believed in beginning at the bottom of the ladder. But he also gave, by his view of Scripture and Science, and other questions, a sort of charter for pioneers more purely practical than himself. He practically said that if they could really prove their practical discoveries, the traditional interpretation of Scripture must give way before those discoveries. He could hardly, as the common phrase goes, say fairer than that. If the matter had been left to him, and men like him, there never would have been any quarrel between Science and Religion. He did his very best to map out two provinces for them, and to trace a just frontier between them.

It is often cheerfully remarked that Christianity has failed, by which is meant that it has never had that sweeping, imperial and imposed supremacy, which has belonged to each of the great revolutions, every one of which has subsequently failed. There was never a moment when men could say that every man was a Christian; as they might say for several months that every man was a Royalist or a Republican or a Communist. But if sane historians want to understand the sense in which the Christian character has succeeded, they could not find a better case than the massive moral pressure of a man like St. Thomas, in support of the buried rationalism of the heathens, which had as yet only been dug up for the amusement of the heretics. It was, quite strictly and exactly, because a new kind of man was conducting rational enquiry in a new kind of way, that men forgot the curse that had fallen on the temples of the dead demons and the palaces of the dead despots; forgot even the new fury out of Arabia against which they were fighting for their lives; because the man who was asking them to return to sense, or to return to their senses, was not a sophist but a saint. Aristotle had described the magnanimous man, who is great and knows that he is great. But Aristotle would never have recovered his own greatness, but for the miracle that created the more magnanimous man; who is great and knows that he is small.

There is a certain historical importance in what some would call the heaviness of the style employed. It carries a curious impression of candour, which really did have, I think, a considerable effect upon contemporaries. The saint has sometimes been called a sceptic. The truth is that he was very largely tolerated as a sceptic because he was obviously a saint. When he seemed to stand up as a stubborn Aristotelian, hardly distinguishable from the Arabian heretics, I do seriously believe that what protected him was very largely the prodigious power of his simplicity and his obvious goodness and love of truth. Those who went out against the haughty confidence of the heretics were stopped and brought up all standing, against a sort of huge humility which was like a mountain: or perhaps like that immense valley that is the mould of a mountain. Allowing for all medieval conventions, we can feel that with the other innovators, this was not always so. The others, from Abelard down to Siger of Brabant, have never quite lost, in the long process of history, a faint air of showing off. Nobody could feel for a moment that Thomas Aquinas was showing off. The very dullness of diction, of which some complain, was enormously convincing. He could have given wit as well as wisdom; but he was so prodigiously in earnest that he gave his wisdom without his wit.

After the hour of triumph came the moment of peril. It is always so with alliances, and especially because Aquinas was fighting on two fronts. His main business was to defend the Faith against the abuse of Aristotle; and he boldly did it by supporting the use of Aristotle. He knew perfectly well that armies of atheists and anarchists were roaring applause in the background at his Aristotelian victory over all he held most dear. Nevertheless, it was never the existence of atheists, any more than Arabs or Aristotelian pagans, that disturbed the extraordinary controversial composure of Thomas Aquinas. The real peril that followed on the victory he had won for Aristotle was vividly presented in the curious case of Siger of Brabant; and it is well worth study, for anyone who would begin to comprehend the strange history of Christendom. It is marked by one rather queer quality; which has always been the unique note of the Faith, though it is not noticed by its modern enemies, and rarely by its modern friends. It is the fact symbolised in the legend of Antichrist, who was the double of Christ; in the profound proverb that the Devil is the ape of God. It is the fact that falsehood is never so false as when it is very nearly true. It is when the stab comes near the nerve of truth, that the Christian conscience cries out in pain. And Siger of Brabant, following on some of the Arabian Aristotelians, advanced a theory which most modern newspaper readers would instantly have declared to be the same as the theory of St. Thomas. That was what finally roused St. Thomas to his last and most emphatic protest. He had won his battle for a wider scope of philosophy and science; he had cleared the ground for a general understanding about faith and enquiry; an understanding that has generally been observed among Catholics, and certainly never deserted without disaster. It was the idea that the scientist should go on exploring and experimenting freely, so long as he did not claim an infallibility and finality which it was against his own principles to claim. Meanwhile the Church should go on developing and defining, about supernatural things, so long as she did not claim a right to alter the deposit of faith, which it was against her own principles to claim. And when he had said this, Siger of Brabant got up and said something so horribly like it, and so horribly unlike, that (like the Antichrist) he might have deceived the very elect.

Siger of Brabant said this: the Church must be right theologically, but she can be wrong scientifically. There are two truths; the truth of the supernatural world, and the truth of the natural world, which contradicts the supernatural world. While we are being naturalists, we can suppose that Christianity is all nonsense; but then, when we remember that we are Christians, we must admit that Christianity is true even if it is nonsense. In other words, Siger of Brabant split the human head in two, like the blow in an old legend of battle; and declared that a man has two minds, with one of which he must entirely believe and with the other may utterly disbelieve. To many this would at least seem like a parody of Thomism. As a fact, it was the assassination of Thomism. It was not two ways of finding the same truth; it was an untruthful way of pretending that there are two truths. And it is extraordinarily interesting to note that this is the one occasion when the Dumb Ox really came out like a wild bull. When he stood up to answer Siger of Brabant, he was altogether transfigured, and the very style of his sentences, which is a thing like the tone of a man's voice, is suddenly altered. He had never been angry with any of the enemies who disagreed with him. But these enemies had attempted the worst treachery: they had made him agree with them.

Those who complain that theologians draw fine distinctions could hardly find a better example of their own folly. In fact, a fine distinction can be a flat contradiction. It was notably so in this case. St. Thomas was willing to allow the one truth to be approached by two paths, precisely *because* he was sure there was only one truth. Because the Faith was the one truth, nothing discovered in nature could ultimately contradict the Faith. Because the Faith was the one truth, nothing really deduced from the Faith could ultimately contradict the facts. It was in truth a curiously daring confidence in the reality of his religion: and though some may linger to dispute it, it has been justified. The scientific facts, which were supposed to contradict the Faith in the nineteenth century, are nearly all of them regarded as unscientific fictions in the twentieth century. Even the materialists have fled from materialism; and those who lectured us about determinism in psychology are already talking about indeterminism in matter. But whether his confidence was right or wrong, it was specially and supremely a confidence that there is one truth which cannot contradict itself. And this last group of enemies suddenly sprang up, to tell him they entirely agreed with him in saying that there are two contradictory truths. Truth, in the medieval phrase, carried two faces under one hood; and these double-faced sophists practically dared to suggest that it was the Dominican hood.

So, in his last battle and for the first time, he fought as with a battle-axe. There is a ring in the words altogether beyond the almost impersonal patience he maintained in debate with so many enemies. "Behold our refutation of the error. It is not based on documents of faith, but on the reasons and statements of the philosophers themselves. If then anyone there be who, boastfully taking pride in his supposed wisdom, wishes to challenge what we have written, let him not do it in some corner nor before children who are powerless to decide on such difficult matters. Let him reply openly if he dare. He shall find me then confronting him, and not only my negligible self, but many another whose study is truth. We shall do battle with his errors or bring a cure to his ignorance."

The Dumb Ox is bellowing now; like one at bay and yet terrible and towering over all the baying pack. We have already noted why, in this one quarrel with Siger of Brabant, Thomas Aquinas let loose such thunders of purely moral passion; it was because the whole work of his life was being betrayed behind his back, by those who had used his victories over the reactionaries. The point at the moment is that this is perhaps his one moment of personal passion, save for a single flash in the troubles of his youth: and he is once more fighting his enemies with a firebrand. And yet, even in this isolated apocalypse of anger, there is one phrase that may be commended for all time to men who are angry with much less cause. If there is one sentence that could be carved in marble, as representing the calmest and most enduring rationality of his unique intelligence, it is a sentence which came pouring out with all the rest of this molten lava. If there is one phrase that stands before history as typical of Thomas Aquinas, it is that phrase about his own argument: "It is not based on documents of faith, but on the reasons and statements of the philosophers themselves." Would that all Orthodox doctors in deliberation were as reasonable as Aquinas in anger! Would that all Christian apologists would remember that maxim; and write it up in large letters on the wall, before they nail any theses there. At the top of his fury, Thomas Aquinas understands, what so many defenders of orthodoxy will not understand. It is no good to tell an atheist that he is an atheist; or to charge a denier of immortality with the infamy of denying it; or to imagine that one can force an opponent to admit he is wrong, by proving that he is wrong on somebody else's principles, but not on his own. After the great example of St. Thomas, the principle stands, or ought always to have stood established; that we must either not argue with a man at all, or we must argue on his grounds and not ours. We may do other things instead of arguing, according to our views of what actions are morally permissible; but if we argue we must argue "On the reasons and statements of the philosophers themselves." This is the common sense in a saying attributed to a friend of St. Thomas, the great St. Louis, King of France, which shallow people quote as a sample of fanaticism; the sense of which is, that I must either argue with an infidel as a real philosopher can argue, or else "thrust a sword through his body as far as it will go." A real philosopher (even of the opposite school) will be the first to agree that St. Louis was entirely philosophical.

So, in the last great controversial crisis of his theological campaign, Thomas Aquinas contrived to give his friends and enemies not only a lesson in theology, but a lesson in controversy. But it was in fact his last controversy. He had been a man with a huge controversial appetite, a thing that exists in some men and not others, in saints and in sinners. But after this great and victorious duel with Siger of Brabant, he was suddenly overwhelmed with a desire for silence and repose. He said one strange thing about this mood of his to a friend, which will fall into its more appropriate place elsewhere. He fell back on the extreme simplicities of his monastic round and seemed to desire nothing but a sort of permanent retreat. A request came to him from the Pope that he should set out upon some further mission of diplomacy or disputation; and he made ready to obey. But before he had gone many miles on the journey, he was dead.

CHAPTER IV

A MEDITATION ON THE MANICHEES

There is one casual anecdote about St. Thomas Aquinas which illuminates him like a lightning-flash, not only without but within. For it not only shows him as a character, and even as a comedy character, and shows the colours of his period and social background; but also, as if for an instant, makes a transparency of his mind. It is a trivial incident which occurred one day, when he was reluctantly dragged from his work, and we might almost say from his play. For both were for him found in the unusual hobby of thinking, which is for some men a thing much more intoxicating than mere drinking. He had declined any number of society invitations, to the courts of kings and princes, not because he was unfriendly, for he was not; but because he was always glowing within with the really gigantic plans of exposition and argument which filled his life. On one occasion, however, he was invited to the court of King Louis IX of France, more famous as the great St. Louis; and for some reason or other, the Dominican authorities of his Order told him to accept; so he immediately did so, being an obedient friar even in his sleep; or rather in his permanent trance of reflection.

It is a real case against conventional hagiography that it sometimes tends to make all saints seem to be the same. Whereas in fact no men are more different than saints; not even murderers. And there could hardly be a more complete contrast, given the essentials of holiness, than between St. Thomas and St. Louis. St. Louis was born a knight and a king; but he was one of those men in whom a certain simplicity, combined with courage and activity, makes it natural, and in a sense easy, to fulfil directly and promptly any duty or office, however official. He was a man in whom holiness and healthiness had no quarrel; and their issue was in action. He did not go in for thinking much, in the sense of theorising much. But, even in theory, he had that sort of presence of mind, which belongs to the rare and really practical man when he has to think. He never said the wrong thing; and he was orthodox by instinct. In the old pagan proverb about kings being philosophers or philosophers kings, there was a certain miscalculation, connected with a mystery that only Christianity could reveal. For while it is possible for a king to wish much to be a saint, it is not possible for a saint to wish very much to be a king. A good man will hardly be always dreaming of being a great monarch; but, such is the liberality of the Church, that she cannot forbid even a great monarch to dream of being a good man. But Louis was a straight-forward soldierly sort of person who did not particularly mind being a king, any more than he would have minded being a captain or a sergeant or any other rank in his army. Now a man like St. Thomas would definitely dislike being a king, or being entangled with the pomp and politics of kings; not only his humility, but a sort of subconscious fastidiousness and fine dislike of futility, often found in leisurely and learned men with large minds, would really have prevented him making contact with the complexity of court life. Also, he was anxious all his life to keep out of politics; and there was no political symbol more striking, or in a sense more challenging, at that moment, than the power of the King in Paris.

Paris was truly at that time an *aurora borealis*; a Sunrise in the North. We must realise that lands much nearer to Rome had rotted with paganism and pessimism and Oriental influences of which the most respectable was that of Mahound. Provence and all the South had been full of a fever of nihilism or negative mysticism, and from Northern France had come the spears and swords that swept away the unchristian thing. In Northern France also sprang up that splendour of building that shine like swords and spears: the first spires of the Gothic. We talk now of grey Gothic buildings; but they must have been very different when they went up white and gleaming into the northern skies, partly picked out with gold and bright colours; a new flight of architecture, as startling as flying-ships. The new Paris ultimately left behind by St. Louis must have been a thing white like lilies and splendid as the oriflamme. It was the beginning of the great new thing: the nation of France, which was to pierce and overpower the old quarrel of Pope and Emperor in the lands from which Thomas came. But Thomas came very unwillingly, and, if we may say it of so kindly a man, rather sulkily. As he entered Paris they showed him from the hill that splendour of new spires beginning, and somebody said something like, "How grand it must be to own all this." And Thomas Aquinas only muttered, "I would rather have that Chrysostom MS. I can't get hold of."

Somehow they steered that reluctant bulk of reflection to a seat in the royal banquet hall; and all that we know of Thomas tells us that he was perfectly courteous to those who spoke to him, but spoke little, and was soon forgotten in the most brilliant and noisy clatter in the world: the noise of French talking. What the Frenchmen were talking about we do not know; but they forgot all about the large fat Italian in their midst, and it seems only too possible that he forgot all about them. Sudden silences will occur even in French conversation; and in one of these the interruption came. There had long been no word or motion in that huge heap of black and white weeds, like motley in mourning, which marked him as a mendicant friar out of the streets, and contrasted with all the colours and patterns and quarterings of that first and freshest dawn of chivalry and heraldry. The triangular shields and pennons and pointed spears, the triangular swords of the Crusade, the pointed windows and the conical hoods, repeated everywhere that fresh French medieval spirit that did, in every sense, come to the point. But the colours of the coats were gay and varied, with little to rebuke their richness; for St. Louis, who had himself a special quality of coming to the point, had said to his courtiers, "Vanity should be avoided; but every man should dress well, in the manner of his rank, that his wife may the more easily love him."

And then suddenly the goblets leapt and rattled on the board and the great table shook, for the friar had brought down his huge fist like a club of stone, with a crash that startled everyone like an explosion; and had cried out in a strong voice, but like a man in the grip of a dream, "And *that* will settle the Manichees!"

The palace of a king, even when it is the palace of a saint, has it conventions. A shock thrilled through the court, and every one felt as if the fat friar from Italy had thrown a plate at King Louis, or knocked his crown sideways. They all looked timidly at the terrible seat, that was for a thousand years the throne of the Capets: and many there were presumably prepared to pitch the big black-robed beggarman out of the window. But St. Louis, simple as he seemed, was no mere medieval fountain of honour or even fountain of mercy but also the fountain of two eternal rivers: the irony and the courtesy of France. And he turned to his secretaries, asking them in a low voice to take their tablets round to the sear of the absent-minded controversialist, and take a note of the argument that had just occurred to him; because it must be a very good one and he might forget it. I have paused upon this anecdote, first, as has been said, because it is the one which gives us the most vivid snapshot of a great medieval character; indeed of two great medieval characters. But it also specially fitted to be taken as a type or a turning-point, because of the glimpse it gives of the man's main preoccupation; and the sort of thing that might have been found in his thoughts, if they had been thus surprised at any moment by a philosophical eavesdropper or through a psychological keyhole. It was not for nothing that he was still brooding, even in the white court of St. Louis, upon the dark cloud of the Manichees.

This book is meant only to be the sketch of a man; but it must at least lightly touch, later on, upon a method and a meaning; or what our journalism has an annoying way of calling a message. A few very inadequate pages must be given to the man in relation to his theology and his philosophy; but the thing of which I mean to speak here is something at once more general and more personal even than his philosophy. I have therefore introduced it here, before we come to anything like technical talk about his philosophy. It was something that might alternatively be called his moral attitude, or his temperamental predisposition, or the purpose of his life so far as social and human effects were concerned: for he knew better than most of us that there is but one purpose in this life, and it is one that is beyond this life. But if we wanted to put in a picturesque and simplified form what he wanted for the world, and what was his work in history, apart from theoretical and theological definitions, we might well say that it really was to strike a blow and settle the Manichees.

The full meaning of this may not be apparent to those who do not study theological history and perhaps even less apparent to those who do. Indeed it may seem equally irrelevant to the history and the theology. In history St. Dominic and Simon de Montfort between them had already pretty well settled the Manichees. And in theology of course an encyclopaedic doctor like Aquinas dealt with a thousand other heresies besides the Manichean heresy. Nevertheless, it does represent his main position and the turn he gave to the whole history of Christendom.

I think it well to interpose this chapter, though its scope may seem more vague than the rest; because there is a sort of big blunder about St. Thomas and his creed, which is an obstacle for most modern people in even beginning to understand them. It arises roughly thus. St. Thomas, like other monks, and especially other saints, lived a life of renunciation and austerity; his fasts, for instance, being in marked contrast to the luxury in which he might have lived if he chose. This element stands high in his religion, as a manner of asserting the will against the power of nature, of thanking the Redeemer by partially sharing his sufferings, of making a man ready for anything as a missionary or martyr, and similar ideals. These happen to be rare in the modern industrial society of the West, outside his communion; and it is therefore assumed that they are the whole meaning of that communion. Because it is uncommon for an alderman to fast for forty days, or a politician to take a Trappist vow of silence, or a man about town to live a life of strict celibacy, the average outsider is convinced, not only that Catholicism is nothing except asceticism, but that asceticism is nothing except pessimism. He is so obliging as to explain to Catholics why they hold this heroic virtue in respect; and is ever ready to point out that the philosophy behind it is an Oriental hatred of anything connected with Nature, and a purely Schopenhauerian disgust with the Will to Live. I read in a "high-class" review of Miss Rebecca West's book on St.. Augustine, the astounding statement that the Catholic Church regards sex as having the nature of sin. How marriage can be a sacrament if sex is a sin, or why it is the Catholics who are in favour of birth and their foes who are in favour of birth-control, I will leave the critic to worry out for himself. My concern is not with that part of the argument; but with another.

The ordinary modern critic, seeing this ascetic ideal in an authoritative Church, and not seeing it in most other inhabitants of Brixton or Brighton, is apt to say, "This is the result of Authority; it would be better to have Religion without Authority." But in truth, a wider experience outside Brixton or Brighton would reveal the mistake. It is rare to find a fasting alderman or a Trappist politician, but it is still more rare to see nuns suspended in the air on hooks or spikes; it is unusual for a Catholic Evidence Guild orator in Hyde Park to begin his speech by gashing himself all over with knives; a stranger calling at an ordinary presbytery will seldom find the parish priest lying on the floor with a fire lighted on his chest and scorching him while he utters spiritual ejaculations. Yet all these things are done all over Asia, for instance, by voluntary enthusiasts acting solely on the great impulse of Religion; of Religion, in their case, not commonly imposed by any immediate Authority; and certainly not imposed by this particular Authority. In short, a real knowledge of mankind will tell anybody that Religion is a very terrible thing; that it is truly a raging fire, and that Authority is often quite as much needed to restrain it as to impose it. Asceticism, or the war with the appetites, is itself an appetite. It can never be eliminated from among the strange ambitions of Man. But it can be kept in some reasonable control; and it is indulged in much saner proportion under Catholic Authority than in Pagan or Puritan anarchy. Meanwhile, the whole of this ideal, though an essential part of Catholic idealism when it is understood, is in some ways entirely a side issue. It is not the primary principle of Catholic philosophy; it is only a particular deduction from Catholic ethics. And when we begin to talk about primary philosophy, we realise the full and flat contradiction between the monk fasting and the fakir hanging himself on hooks.

Now nobody will begin to understand the Thomist philosophy, or indeed the Catholic philosophy, who does not realise that the primary and fundamental part of it is entirely the praise of Life, the praise of Being, the praise of God as the Creator of the World. Everything else follows a long way after that, being conditioned by various complications like the Fall or the vocation of heroes. The trouble occurs because the Catholic mind moves upon two planes; that of the Creation and that of the Fall. The nearest parallel is, for instance, that of England invaded; there might be strict martial law in Kent because the enemy had landed in Kent, and relative liberty in Hereford; but this would not affect the affection of an English patriot for Hereford or Kent, and strategic caution in Kent would not affect the love of Kent. For the love of England would remain, both the parts to be redeemed by discipline and the parts to be enjoyed in liberty. Any extreme of Catholic asceticism is a wise, or unwise, precaution against the evil of the Fall; it is *never* a doubt about the good of the Creation. And *that* is where it really does differ, nor only from the rather excessive eccentricity of the gentleman who hangs himself on hooks, but from the whole cosmic theory which is the hook on which he hangs. In the case of many Oriental religions, it really is true that the asceticism is pessimism; that the ascetic tortures himself to death out of an abstract hatred of life; that he does nor merely mean to control Nature as he should, but to contradict Nature as much as he can. And though it takes a milder form than hooks in millions of the religious populations of Asia, it is a fact far too little realised, that the dogma of the denial of life does really rule as a first principle on so vast a scale. One historic form it took was that great enemy of Christianity from its beginnings: the Manichees.

What is called the Manichean philosophy has had many forms; indeed it has attacked what is immortal and immutable with a very curious kind of immortal mutability. It is like the legend of the magician who turns himself into a snake or a cloud; and the whole has that nameless note of irresponsibility, which belongs to much of the metaphysics and morals of Asia, from which the Manichean mystery came. But it is always in one way or another a notion that nature is evil; or that evil is at least rooted in nature. The essential point is that as evil has roots in nature, so it has rights in nature. Wrong has as much right to exist as right. As already stated this notion took many forms. Sometimes it was a dualism, which made evil an equal partner with good; so that neither could be called an usurper. More often it was a general idea that demons had made the material world, and if there were any good spirits, they were concerned only with the spiritual world. Later, again, it took the form of Calvinism, which held that God had indeed made the world, but in a special sense, made the evil as well as the good: had made an evil will as well as an evil world. On this view, if a man chooses to damn his soul alive, he is not thwarting God's will but rather fulfilling it. In these two forms, of the early Gnosticism and the later Calvinism, we see the superficial variety and fundamental unity of Manicheanism. The old Manicheans taught that Satan originated the whole work of creation commonly attributed to God. The new Calvinists taught that God originates the whole work of damnation commonly attributed to Satan. One looked back to the first day when a devil acted like a god, the other looked forward to a last day when a god acted like a devil. But both had the idea that the creator of the earth was primarily the creator of the evil, whether we call him a devil or a god.

Since there are a good many Manicheans among the Moderns, as we may remark in a moment, some may agree with this view, some may be puzzled about it, some may only be puzzled about why we should object to it. To understand the medieval controversy, a word must be said of the Catholic doctrine, which is as modern as it is medieval. That "God looked on all things and saw that they were good" contains a subtlety which the popular pessimist cannot follow, or is too hasty to notice. It is the thesis that there are no bad things, but only bad uses of things. If you will, there are no bad things but only bad thoughts; and especially bad intentions. Only Calvinists can really believe that hell is paved with good intentions. That is exactly the one thing it cannot be paved with. But it is possible to have bad intentions about good things; and good things, like the world and the flesh have been twisted by a bad intention called the devil. But he cannot make *things* bad; they remain as on the first day of creation. The work of heaven alone was material; the making of a material world. The work of hell is entirely spiritual.

This error then had many forms; but especially, like nearly every error, it had two forms, a fiercer one which was outside the Church and attacking the Church, and a subtler one, which was inside the Church and corrupting the Church. There has never been a time when the Church was not torn between that invasion and that treason. It was so, for instance, in the Victorian time, Darwinian "competition," in commerce or race conflict, was every bit as brazen an atheist assault, in the nineteenth century, as the Bolshevist No-God movement in the twentieth century. To brag of brute prosperity, to admire the most muddly millionaires who had cornered wheat by a trick, to talk about the "unfit" (in imitation of the scientific thinker who would finish them off because he cannot even finish his own sentence— unfit for what?)—all that is as simply and openly Anti-Christian as the Black Mass. Yet some weak and worldly Catholics did use this cant in defence of Capitalism, in their first rather feeble resistance to Socialism. At least they did until the great Encyclical of the Pope on the Rights of Labour put a stop to all their nonsense. The evil is always both within and without the Church; but in a wilder form outside and a milder form inside. So it was, again, in the seventeenth century, when there was Calvinism outside and Jansenism inside. And so it was in the thirteenth century, when the obvious danger outside was in the revolution of the Albigensians; but the potential danger inside was in the very traditionalism of the Augustinians. For the Augustinians derived only from Augustine, and Augustine derived partly from Plato, and Plato was right, but not quite right. It is a mathematical fact that if a line be not perfectly directed towards a point, it will actually go further away from it as it comes nearer to it. After a thousand years of extension, the miscalculation of Platonism had come very near to Manicheanism.

Popular errors are nearly always right. They nearly always refer to some ultimate reality, about which those who correct them are themselves incorrect. It is a very queer thing that "Platonic Love" has come to mean for the unlettered something rather purer and cleaner than it means for the learned. Yet even those who realise the great Greek evil may well realise that perversity often comes out of the wrong sort of purity. Now it was the inmost lie of the Manichees that they identified purity with sterility. It is singularly contrasted with the language of St. Thomas, which always connects purity with fruitfulness; whether it be natural or supernatural. And, queerly enough, as I have said, there does remain a sort of reality in the vulgar colloquialism that the affair between Sam and Susan is "quite Platonic." It is true that, quite apart from the local perversion, there was in Plato a sort of idea that people would be better without their bodies: that their heads might fly off and meet in the sky in merely intellectual marriage, like cherubs in a picture. The ultimate phase of this "Platonic" philosophy was what inflamed poor D. H. Lawrence into talking nonsense, and he was probably unaware that the Catholic doctrine of marriage would say much of what he said, without talking nonsense. Anyhow, it is historically important to see that Platonic love did somewhat distort both human and divine love, in the theory of the early theologians. Many medieval men, who would indignantly deny the Albigensian doctrine of sterility, were yet in an emotional mood to abandon the body in despair; and some of them to abandon everything in despair.

In truth, this vividly illuminates the provincial stupidity of those who object to what they call "creeds and dogmas." It was precisely the creed and dogma that saved the sanity of the world. These people generally propose an alternative religion of intuition and feeling. If, in the really Dark Ages, there had been a religion of feeling, it would have been a religion of black and suicidal feeling. It was the rigid creed that resisted the rush of suicidal feeling. The critics of asceticism are probably right in supposing that many a Western hermit did *feel* rather like an Eastern fakir. But he could not really *think* like an Eastern fakir; because he was an orthodox Catholic. And what kept his thought in touch with healthier and more humanistic thought was simply and solely the Dogma. He could not deny that a good God had created the normal and natural world; he could not say that the devil had made the world; because he was not a Manichee. A thousand enthusiasts for celibacy, in the day of the great rush to the desert or the cloister, might have called marriage a sin, if they had only considered their individual ideals, in the modern manner, and their own immediate feelings about marriage. Fortunately, they had to accept the Authority of the Church, which had definitely said that marriage was not a sin. A modern emotional religion might at any moment have turned Catholicism into Manichaeism. But when Religion would have maddened men, Theology kept them sane.

In this sense St. Thomas stands up simply as the great orthodox theologian, who reminded men of the creed of Creation, when many of them were still in the mood of mere destruction. It is futile for the critics of medievalism to quote a hundred medieval phrases that may be supposed to sound like mere pessimism, if they will not understand the central fact; that medieval men did not care about being medieval and did not accept the authority of a mood, because it was melancholy, but did care very much about orthodoxy, which is not a mood. It was because St. Thomas could *prove* that his glorification of the Creator and His creative joy was more orthodox than any atmospheric pessimism, that he dominated the Church and the world, which accepted that truth as a test. But when this immense and impersonal importance is allowed for, we may agree that there was a personal element as well. Like most of the great religious teachers, he was fitted individually for the task that God had given him to do. We can if we like call that talent instinctive; we can even descend to calling it temperamental.

Anybody trying to popularise a medieval philosopher must use language that is very modern and very unphilosophical. Nor is this a sneer at modernity;

it arises from the moderns having dealt so much in moods and emotions, especially in the arts, that they have developed a large but loose vocabulary, which deals more with atmosphere than with actual attitude or position. As noted elsewhere, even the modern philosophers are more like the modern poets; in giving an individual tinge even to truth, and often looking at all life through different coloured spectacles. To say that Schopenhauer had the blues, or that William James had a rather rosier outlook, would often convey more than calling the one a Pessimist or the other a Pragmatist. This modern moodiness has its value, though the moderns overrate it; just as medieval logic had its value, though it was overrated in the later Middle Ages. But the point is that to explain the medievals to the moderns, we must often use this modern language of mood. Otherwise the character will be missed, through certain prejudices and ignorances about all such medieval characters. Now there is something that lies all over the work of St. Thomas Aquinas like a great light: which is something quite primary and perhaps unconscious with him, which he would perhaps have passed over as an irrelevant personal quality; and which can now only be expressed by a rather cheap journalistic term, which he would probably have thought quite senseless.

Nevertheless, the only working word for that atmosphere is Optimism. I know that the word is now even more degraded in the twentieth century than it was in the nineteenth century. Men talked lately of being Optimists about the issue of War; they talk now of being Optimists about the revival of Trade; they may talk tomorrow of being Optimists about the International Ping-pong Tournament. But men in the Victorian time did mean a little more than that, when they used the word Optimist of Browning or Stevenson or Walt Whitman. And in a rather larger and more luminous sense than in the case of these men, the term was basically true of Thomas Aquinas. He did, with a most solid and colossal conviction, believe in Life: and in something like what Stevenson called the great theorem of the livableness of life. It breathes somehow in his very first phrases about the reality of Being. If the morbid Renaissance intellectual is supposed to say, "To be or not to be— that is the question," then the massive medieval doctor does most certainly reply in a voice of thunder, "To be—that is the answer." The point is important; many not unnaturally talk of the Renaissance as the time when certain men began to believe in Life. The truth is that it was the time when a few men, for the first time, began to disbelieve in Life. The medievals had put many restrictions, and some excessive restrictions, upon the universal human hunger and even fury for Life. Those restrictions had often been expressed in fanatical and rabid terms; the terms of those resisting a great natural force; the force of men who desired to live. Never until modern thought began, did they really have to fight with men who desired to die. That horror had threatened them in Asiatic Albigensianism, but it never became normal to them—until now.

But this fact becomes very vivid indeed, when we compare the greatest of Christian philosophers with the only men who were anything like his equals, or capable of being his rivals. They were people with whom he did not directly dispute; most of them he had never seen; some of them he had never heard of. Plato and Augustine were the only two with whom he could confer as he did with Bonaventure or even Averrhoes. But we must look elsewhere for his real rivals, and the only real rivals of the Catholic theory. They are the heads of great heathen systems; some of them very ancient, some very modern, like Buddha on the one hand or Nietzsche on the other. It is when we see his gigantic figure against this vast and cosmic background, that we realise, first, that he was the only optimist theologian, and second, that Catholicism is the only optimist theology. Something milder and more amiable may be made out of the deliquescence of theology, and the mixture of the creed with everything that contradicts it; but among consistent cosmic creeds, this is the only one that is entirely on the side of Life.

Comparative religion has indeed allowed us to compare religions— and to contrast them. Fifty years ago, it set out to prove that all religions were much the same; generally proving, alternately, that they were all equally worthy and that they were all equally worthless. Since then this scientific process has suddenly begun to be scientific, and discovered the depths of the chasms as well as the heights of the hills. It is indeed an excellent improvement that sincerely religious people should respect each other. But respect has discovered difference, where contempt knew only indifference. The more we really appreciate the noble revulsion and renunciation of Buddha, the more we see that intellectually it was the converse and almost the contrary of the salvation of the world by Christ. The Christian would escape from the world into the universe: the Buddhist wishes to escape from the universe even more than from the world. One would uncreate himself; the other would return to his Creation: to his Creator. Indeed it was so genuinely the converse of the idea of the Cross as the Tree of Life, that there is some excuse for setting up the two things side by side, as if they were of equal significance. They are in one sense parallel and equal; as a mound and a hollow, as a valley and a hill. There is a sense in which that sublime despair is the only alternative to that divine audacity. It is even true that the truly spiritual and intellectual man sees it as a sort of dilemma; a very hard and terrible choice. There is little else on earth that can compare with these for completeness. And he who will not climb the mountain of Christ does indeed fall into the abyss of Buddha.

The same is true, in a less lucid and dignified fashion, of most other alternatives of heathen humanity; nearly all are sucked back into that whirlpool of recurrence which all the ancients knew. Nearly all return to the one idea of returning. That is what Buddha described so darkly as the Sorrowful Wheel. It is true that the sort of recurrence which Buddha described as the Sorrowful Wheel, poor Nietzsche actually managed to describe as the Joyful Wisdom. I can only say that if bare repetition was his idea of Joyful Wisdom, I should be curious to know what was his idea of Sorrowful Wisdom. But as a fact, in the case of Nietzsche, this did not belong to the moment of his breaking out, but to the moment of his breaking down. It came at the end of his life, when he was near to mental collapse; and it is really quite contrary to his earlier and finer inspirations of wild freedom or fresh and creative innovation. Once at least he had tried to break out; but he also was only broken— on the wheel.

Alone upon the earth, and lifted and liberated from all the wheels and whirlpools of the earth, stands up the faith of St. Thomas weighted and balanced indeed with more than Oriental metaphysics and more than Pagan pomp and pageantry; but vitally and vividly alone in declaring that life is a living story, with a great beginning and a great close; rooted in the primeval joy of God and finding its fruition in the final happiness of humanity; opening with the colossal chorus in which the sons of God shouted for joy, and ending in that mystical comradeship, shown in a shadowy fashion in those ancient words that move like an archaic dance; "For His delight is with the sons of men."

It is the fate of this sketch to be sketchy about philosophy, scanty or rather empty about theology, and to achieve little more than a decent silence on the subject of sanctity. And yet it must none the less be the recurrent burden of this little book, to which it must return with some monotony, that in this story the philosophy did depend on the theology, and the theology did depend on the sanctity. In other words, it must repeat the first fact, which was emphasised in the first chapter: that this great intellectual creation was a Christian and Catholic creation and cannot be understood as anything else. It was Aquinas who baptised Aristotle, when Aristotle could not have baptised Aquinas; it was a purely Christian miracle which raised the great Pagan from the dead. And this is proved in three ways (as St. Thomas himself might say), which it will be well to summarise as a sort of summary of this book.

First, in the life of St. Thomas, it is proved in the fact that only his huge and solid orthodoxy could have supported so many things which then seemed to be unorthodox. Charity covers a multitude of sins; and in that sense orthodoxy covers a multitude of heresies; or things which are hastily mistaken for heresies. It was precisely because his personal Catholicism was so convincing, that his impersonal Aristotelianism was given the benefit of the doubt. He did not smell of the faggot because he did smell of the firebrand; of the firebrand he had so instantly and instinctively snatched up, under a real assault on essential Catholic ethics. A typically cynical modern phrase refers to the man who is so good that he is good for nothing. St. Thomas was so good that he was good for everything; that his warrant held good for what others considered the most wild and daring speculations, ending in the worship of nothing. Whether or no he baptised Aristotle, he was truly the godfather of Aristotle, he was his sponsor; he swore that the old Greek would do no harm; and the whole world trusted his word.

Second, in the philosophy of St. Thomas, it is proved by the fact that everything depended on the new Christian *motive* for the study of facts, as distinct from truths. The Thomist philosophy began with the lowest roots of thought, the senses and the truisms of the reason; and a Pagan sage might have scorned such things, as he scorned the servile arts. But the materialism, which is merely cynicism in a Pagan, can be Christian humility in a Christian. St. Thomas was willing to begin by recording the facts and sensations of the material world, just as he would have been willing to begin by washing up the plates and dishes in the monastery. The point of his Aristotelianism was that even if common sense about concrete things really was a sort of servile labour, he must not be ashamed to be *servus servorum Dei*. Among heathens the mere sceptic might become the mere cynic; Diogenes in his tub had always a touch of the tub-thumper; but even the dirt of the cynics was dignified into dust and ashes among the saints. If we miss that, we miss the whole meaning of the greatest revolution in history. There was a new *motive* for beginning with the most material, and even with the meanest things.

Third, in the theology of St. Thomas, it is proved by the tremendous truth that supports all that theology; or any other Christian theology. There really was a new reason for regarding the senses, and the sensations of the body, and the experiences of the common man, with a reverence at which great Aristotle would have stared, and no man in the ancient world could have begun to understand. The Body was no longer what it was when Plato and Porphyry and the old mystics had left it for dead. It had hung upon a gibbet. It had risen from a tomb. It was no longer possible for the soul to despise the senses, which had been the organs of something that was more than man. Plato might despise the flesh; but God had not despised it. The senses had truly become sanctified; as they are blessed one by one at a Catholic baptism. "Seeing is believing" was no longer the platitude of a mere idiot, or common individual, as in Plato's world; it was mixed up with real conditions of real belief. Those revolving mirrors that send messages to the brain of man, that light that breaks upon the brain, these had truly revealed to God himself the path to Bethany or the light on the high rock of Jerusalem. These ears that resound with common noises had reported also to the secret knowledge of God the noise of the crowd that strewed palms and the crowd that cried for Crucifixion. After the Incarnation had become the idea that is central in our civilisation, it was inevitable that there should be a return to materialism, in the sense of the serious value of matter and the making of the body. When once Christ had risen, it was inevitable that Aristotle should rise again.

Those are three real reasons, and very sufficient reasons, for the general support given by the saint to a solid and objective philosophy. And yet there was something else, very vast and vague, to which I have tried to give a faint expression by the interposition of this chapter. It is difficult to express it fully, without the awful peril of being popular, or what the Modernists quite wrongly imagine to be popular; in short, passing from religion to religiosity. But there is a general tone and temper of Aquinas, which it is as difficult to avoid as daylight in a great house of windows. It is that *positive* position of his mind, which is filled and soaked as with sunshine with the warmth of the wonder of created things. There is a certain private audacity, in his communion, by which men add to their private names the tremendous titles of the Trinity and the Redemption; so that some nun may be called "of the Holy Ghost;" or a man bear such a burden as the title of St. John of the Cross. In this sense, the man we study may specially be called St. Thomas of the Creator. The Arabs have a phrase about the hundred names of God; but they also inherit the tradition of a tremendous name unspeakable because it expresses Being itself, dumb and yet dreadful as an instant inaudible shout; the proclamation of the Absolute. And perhaps no other man ever came so near to calling the Creator by His own name, which can only be written I Am.

CHAPTER V

THE REAL LIFE OF ST. THOMAS

At this point, even so crude and external a sketch of a great saint involves the necessity of writing something that cannot fit in with the rest; the one thing which it is important to write and impossible to write. A saint may be any kind of man, with an additional quality that is at once unique and universal. We might even say that the one thing which separates a saint from ordinary men is his readiness to be one with ordinary men. In this sense the word ordinary must be understood in its native and noble meaning; which is connected with the word order. A saint is long past any desire for distinction; he is the only sort of superior man who has never been a superior person. But all this arises from a great central fact, which he does not condescend to call a privilege, but which is in its very nature a sort of privacy; and in that sense almost a form of private property. As with all sound private property, it is enough for him that he has it, he does not desire to limit the number of people who have it. He is always trying to hide it, out of a sort of celestial good manners; and Thomas Aquinas tried to hide it more than most. To reach it, in so far as we can reach it, it will be best to begin with the upper strata; and reach what was in the inside from what was most conspicuous on the outside.

The appearance or bodily presence of St. Thomas Aquinas is really easier to resurrect than that of many who lived before the age of portrait painting. It has been said that in his bodily being or bearing there was little of the Italian; but this is at the best, I fancy an unconscious comparison between St. Thomas and St. Francis; and at worst, only a comparison between him and the hasty legend of vivacious organ-grinders and incendiary ice-cream men. Not all Italians are vivacious organ-grinders, and very few Italians are like St. Francis. A nation is never a type, but it is nearly always a tangle of two or three roughly recognizable types. St. Thomas was of a certain type, which is not so much common in Italy, as common to uncommon Italians.

His bulk made it easy to regard him humorously as the sort of walking wine-barrel, common in the comedies of many nations: he joked about it himself. It may be that he, and not some irritated partisan of the Augustinian or Arabian parties, was responsible for the sublime exaggeration that a crescent was cut out of the dinner-table to allow him to sit down. It is quite certain that it was an exaggeration; and that his stature was more remarked than his stoutness; but, above all, that his head was quite powerful enough to dominate his body. And his head was of a very real and recognisable type, to judge by the traditional portraits and the personal descriptions. It was that sort of head with the heavy chin and jaws, the Roman nose and the big rather bald brow, which, in spite of its fullness, gives also a curious concave impression of hollows here and there, like caverns of thought. Napoleon carried that head upon a short body. Mussolini carries it today, upon a rather taller but equally active one. It can be seen in the busts of several Roman Emperors, and occasionally above the shabby shirt-front of an Italian waiter; but he is generally a head waiter. So unmistakable is the type, that I cannot but think that the most vivid villain of light fiction, in the Victorian shocker called *The Woman in White*, was really sketched by Wilkie Collins from an actual Italian Count; he is so complete a contrast to the conventional skinny, swarthy and gesticulating villain whom the Victorians commonly presented as an Italian Count. Count Fosco, it may be remembered (I hope) by some, was a calm, corpulent, colossal gentleman, whose head was exactly like a bust of Napoleon of heroic size. He may have been a melodramatic villain; but he was a tolerably convincing Italian—of that kind. If we recall his tranquil manner, and the excellent common sense of his everyday external words and actions, we shall probably have a merely material image of the type of Thomas Aquinas; given only the slight effort of faith required to imagine Count Fosco turned suddenly into a saint.

The pictures of St. Thomas, though many of them were painted long after his death, are all obviously pictures of the same man. He rears himself defiantly, with the Napoleonic head and the dark bulk of body, in Raphael's "Dispute About the Sacrament." A portrait by Ghirlandajo emphasises a point which specially reveals what may be called the neglected Italian quality in the man. It also emphasises points that are very important in the mystic and the philosopher. It is universally attested that Aquinas was what is commonly called an absent-minded man. That type has often been rendered in painting, humorous or serious; but almost always in one of two or three conventional ways. Sometimes the expression of the eyes is merely vacant, as it absent-mindedness did really mean a permanent absence of mind. Sometimes it is rendered more respectfully as a wistful expression, as of one yearning for something afar off, that he cannot see and can only faintly desire. Look at the eves in Ghirlandajo's portrait of St. Thomas; and you will see a sharp difference. While the eyes are indeed completely torn away from the immediate surroundings, so that the pot of flowers above the philosopher's head might fall on it without attracting his attention, they are not in the least wistful, let alone vacant. There is kindled in them a fire of instant inner excitement; they are vivid and very Italian eyes. The man is thinking about something; and something that has reached a crisis; not about nothing or about anything; or, what is almost worse, about everything. There must have been that smouldering vigilance in his eyes, the moment before he smote the table and startled the banquet hall of the King.

Of the personal habits that go with the personal physique, we have also a few convincing and confirming impressions. When he was not sitting still, reading a book, he walked round and round the cloisters and walked fast and even furiously, a very characteristic action of men who fight their battles in the mind. Whenever he was interrupted he was very polite and more apologetic than the apologizer. But there was that about him, which suggested that he was rather happier when he was not interrupted. He was ready to stop his truly Peripatetic tramp: but we feel that when he resumed it, he walked all the faster.

All this suggests that his superficial abstraction, that which the world saw, was of a certain kind. It will be well to understand the quality, for there are several kinds of absence of mind, including that of some pretentious poets and intellectuals, in whom the mind has never been noticeably present. There is the abstraction of the contemplative, whether he is the true sort of Christian contemplative, who is contemplating Something, or the wrong sort of Oriental contemplative, who is contemplating Nothing. Obviously St. Thomas was not a Buddhist mystic; but I do not think his fits of abstraction were even those of a Christian mystic. If he had trances of true Christian mysticism, he took jolly good care that *they* should not occur at other people's dinner-tables. I think he had the sort of bemused fit, which really belongs to the practical man rather than the entirely mystical man. He uses the recognised distinction between the active life and the contemplative life, but in the cases concerned here, I think even his contemplative life was an active life. It had nothing to do with his higher life, in the sense of ultimate sanctity. It rather reminds us that Napoleon would fall into a fit of apparent boredom at the Opera, and afterwards confess that he was thinking how he could get three army corps at Frankfurt to combine with two army corps at Cologne. So, in the case of Aquinas, if his daydreams were dreams, they were dreams of the day; and dreams of the day of battle. If he talked to himself, it was because he was arguing with somebody else. We can put it another way, by saying that his daydreams, like the dreams of a dog, were dreams of hunting; of pursuing the error as well as pursuing the truth; of following all the twists and turns of evasive falsehood, and tracking it at last to its lair in hell. He would have been the first to admit that the erroneous thinker would probably be more surprised to learn where his thought came from, than anybody else to discover where it went to. But this notion of *pursuing* he certainly had, and it was the beginning of a thousand mistakes and misunderstandings that pursuing is called in Latin Persecution. Nobody had less than he had of what is commonly called the temper of a persecutor; but he had the quality which in desperate times is often driven to persecute; and that is simply the sense that everything lives somewhere, and nothing dies unless it dies in its own home. That he did sometimes, in this sense, urge in dreams the shadowy chase even in broad daylight, is quite true. But he was an active dreamer, if not what is commonly called a man of action; and in that chase he was truly to be counted among the *domini canes*; and surely the mightiest and most magnanimous of the Hounds of Heaven.

There may be many who do not understand the nature even of this sort of abstraction. But then, unfortunately, there are many who do not understand the nature of any sort of argument. Indeed, I think there are fewer people now alive who understand argument than there were twenty or thirty years ago; and St. Thomas might have preferred the society of the atheists of the early nineteenth century to that of the blank sceptics of the early twentieth. Anyhow, one of the real disadvantages of the great and glorious sport, that is called argument, is its inordinate length. If you argue honestly, as St. Thomas always did, you will find that the subject sometimes seems as if it would never end. He was strongly conscious of this fact, as appears in many places; for instance his argument that most men must have a revealed religion, because they have not time to argue. No time, that is, to argue fairly. There is always time to argue unfairly; not least in a time like ours. Being himself resolved to argue, to argue honestly, to answer everybody, to deal with everything, he produced books enough to sink a ship or stock a library; though he died in comparatively early middle age. Probably he could not have done it at all, if he had not been thinking even when he was not writing; but above all thinking *combatively*. This, in his case, certainly did not mean bitterly or spitefully or uncharitably; but it did mean combatively. As a matter of fact, it is generally the man who is not ready to argue, who is ready to sneer. That is why, in recent literature, there has been so little argument and so much sneering.

We have noted that there are barely one or two occasions on which St. Thomas indulged in a denunciation. There is not a single occasion on which he indulged in a sneer. His curiously simple character, his lucid but laborious intellect, could not be better summed up than by saying that he did not know how to sneer. He was in a double sense an intellectual aristocrat: but he was never an intellectual snob. He never troubled at all whether those to whom he talked were more or less of the sort whom the world thinks worth talking to: and it was apparent by the impression of his contemporaries that those who received the ordinary scraps of his wit or wisdom were quite as likely to be nobodies as somebodies, or even quite as likely to be noodles as clever people. He was interested in the souls of all his fellow creatures, but not in classifying the minds of any of them; in a sense it was too personal and in another sense too arrogant for his particular mind and temper. He was very much interested in the subject he was talking about; and may sometimes have talked for a long time, though he was probably silent for a much longer time. But he had all the unconscious contempt which the really intelligent have for an intelligentsia.

Like most men concerned with the common problems of men, he seems to have had a considerable correspondence; considering that correspondence was so much more difficult in his time. We have records of a great many cases in which complete strangers wrote to ask him questions, and sometimes rather ridiculous questions. To all of these he replied with a characteristic mixture of patience and that sort of rationality, which in some rational people tends to be impatience. Somebody, for instance, asked him whether the names of all the blessed were written on a scroll exhibited in heaven. He wrote back with untiring calm; "So far as I can see, this is not the case; but there is no harm in saying so."

I have remarked on the portrait of St. Thomas by an Italian painter, which shows him alert even in abstraction; and only silent as if about to speak. Pictures in that great tradition are generally full of small touches that show a very large imagination. I mean the sort of imagination on which Ruskin remarked, when he saw that in Tintoretto's sunlit scene of the Crucifixion the face of Christ is dark and undecipherable; but the halo round his head unexpectedly faint and grey like the colour of ashes. It would be hard to put more powerfully the idea of Divinity itself in eclipse. There is a touch, which it may be fanciful to find equally significant, in the portrait of Thomas Aquinas. The artist, having given so much vividness and vigilance to the eyes, may have felt that he stressed too much the merely combative concentration of the saint; but anyhow for some reason he has blazoned upon his breast a rather curious emblem, as if it were some third symbolic and cyclopean eye. At least it is no normal Christian sign; but something more like the disk of the sun such as held the face of a heathen god; but the face itself is dark and occult, and only the rays breaking from it are a ring of fire. I do not know whether any traditional meaning has been attached to this; but its imaginative meaning is strangely apt. That secret sun, dark with excess of light, or not showing its light save in the enlightenment of others, might well be the exact emblem of that inner and ideal life of the saint, which was not only hidden by his external words and actions, but even hidden by his merely outward and automatic silences and fits of reflection. In short, this spiritual detachment is not to be confused with his common habit of brooding or falling into a brown study. He was a man entirely careless of all casual criticism of his casual demeanour; as are many men built on a big masculine model and unconsciously inheriting a certain social splendour and largesse. But about his real life of sanctity he was intensely secretive. Such secrecy has indeed generally gone with sanctity; for the saint has an unfathomable horror of playing the Pharisee. But in Thomas Aquinas it was even more sensitive, and what many in the world would call morbid. He did not mind being caught wool-gathering over the wine-cups of the King's banquet; for that was merely upon a point of controversy. But when there was some question of his having seen St. Paul in a vision, he was in an agony of alarm lest it should be discussed; and the story remains somewhat uncertain in consequence. Needless to say, his followers and admirers were as eager to collect these strictly miraculous stories as he was eager to conceal them; and one or two seem to be preserved with a fairly solid setting of evidence. But there are certainly fewer of them, known to the world, than in the case of many saints equally sincere and even equally modest, but more preoccupied with zeal and less sensitive about publicity.

The truth is that about all such things, in life and death, there is a sort of enormous quiet hanging about St. Thomas. He was one of those large things who take up little room. There was naturally a certain stir about his miracles after his death; and about his burial at the time when the University of Paris wished to bury him. I do not know in detail the long history of the other plans of sepulture, which have ultimately ended with his sacred bones lying in the church of St. Sernin in Toulouse: at the very base of the battle-fields where his Dominicans had warred down the pestilence of pessimism from the East. But somehow, it is not easy to think of his shrine as the scene of the more jolly, rowdy and vulgar devotion either in its medieval or modern form. He was very far from being a Puritan, in the true sense; he made a provision for a holiday and banquet for his young friends, which has quite a convivial sound. The trend of his writing especially for his time, is reasonable in its recognition of physical life; and he goes out of his way to say that men must vary their lives with jokes and even with pranks. But for all that, we cannot somehow see his personality as a sort of magnet for mobs: or the road to the tomb of St. Thomas at Toulouse having always been a long street of taverns like that to the tomb of St. Thomas at Canterbury. I think he rather disliked noise; there is a legend that he disliked thunderstorms; but it is contradicted by the fact that in an actual shipwreck he was supremely calm. However that may be, and it probably concerned his health, in some ways sensitive, he certainly was very calm. We have a feeling that we should gradually grow conscious of his presence; as of an immense background.

Here, if this slight sketch could be worthy of its subject, there should stand forth something of that stupendous certitude, in the presence of which all his libraries of philosophy, and even theology, were but a litter of pamphlets. It is certain that this thing was in him from the first, in the form of conviction long before it could possibly have even begun to take the form of controversy. It was very vivid in his childhood; and his were exactly the circumstances in which the anecdotes of the nursery and the playground are likely enough to have been really preserved. He had from the first that full and final test of truly orthodox Catholicity; the impetuous, impatient intolerant passion for the poor; and even that readiness to be rather a nuisance to the rich, out of a hunger to feed the hungry. This can have had nothing to do with the intellectualism of which he was afterwards accused; still less with any habit of dialectic. It would seem unlikely that at the age of six he had any ambition to answer Averrhoes or that he knew what Effective Causality is; or even that he had worked out, as he did in later life, the whole theory by which a man's love of himself is Sincere and Constant and Indulgent; and that this should be transferred intact (if possible) to his love of his neighbour. At this early age he did not understand all this. He only did it. But all the atmosphere of his actions carries a sort of conviction with it. It is beautifully typical for instance, of that sort of aristocratic *ménage*, that his parents seem to have objected mildly, if at all, to his handing out things to beggars and tramps; but it was intensely disliked by the upper servants.

Still, if we take the thing as seriously as all childish things should be taken, we may learn something from that mysterious state of innocence, which is the first and best spring of all our later indignations. We may begin to understand why it was that there grew steadily with his growing mind, a great and very solitary mind, an ambition that was the inversion of all the things about him. We shall guess what had continuously swelled within him, whether in protest or prophecy or prayer for deliverance, before he startled his family by flinging away not only the trappings of nobility, but all forms of ambition, even ecclesiastical ambition. His childhood may contain the hint of that first stride of his manhood, from the house onto the highway; and his proclamation that he also would be a Beggar.

There is another case of a sort of second glimpse or sequel, in which an incident well known in the external sense gives us also a glimpse of the internal. After the affair of the firebrand, and the woman who tempted him in the tower, it is said that he had a dream; in which two angels girded him with a cord of fire, a thing of terrible pain and yet giving a terrible strength; and he awoke with a great cry in the darkness. This also has something very vivid about it, under the circumstances; and probably contains truths that will be some day better understood, when priests and doctors have learned to talk to each other without the stale etiquette of nineteenth-century negations. It would be easy to analyse the dream, as the very nineteenth-century doctor did in *Armadale*, resolving it into the details of the past days; the cord from his struggle against being stripped of his Friar's frock; the thread of fire running through the tapestries of the night, from the firebrand he had snatched from the fireside. But even in *Armadale* the dream was fulfilled mystically as well, and the dream of St. Thomas was fulfilled very mystically indeed. For he did in fact remain remarkably untroubled on that side of his human nature after the incident; though it is likely enough that the incident had caused an upheaval of his normal humanity, which produced a dream stronger than a nightmare. This is no place to analyse the psychological fact, which puzzles Non-Catholics so much: of the way in which priests do manage to be celibate without ceasing to be virile. Anyhow, it seems probable that in this matter he was less troubled than most. This has nothing to do with true virtue, which is of the will; saints as holy as he have rolled themselves in brambles to distract the pressure of passion; but he never needed much in the way of a counter-irritant; for the simple reason that in this way, as in most ways, he was not very often irritated. Much must remain unexplained, as part of the mysteries of grace; but there is probably some truth in the psychological idea of "sublimation;" that is the lifting of a lower energy to higher ends; so that appetite almost faded in the furnace of his intellectual energy. Between supernatural and natural causes, it is probable that he never knew or suffered greatly on this side of his mind.

There are moments when the most orthodox reader is tempted to hate the hagiographer as much as he loves the holy man. The holy man always conceals his holiness; that is the one invariable rule. And the hagiographer sometimes seems like a persecutor trying to frustrate the holy man; a spy or eavesdropper hardly more respectful than an American interviewer. I admit that these sentiments are fastidious and one-sided, and I will now proceed to prove my penitence by mentioning one or two of the incidents that could only have come to common knowledge in this deplorable way.

It seems certain that he did live a sort of secondary and mysterious life; the divine double of what is called a double life. Somebody seems to have caught a glimpse of the sort of solitary miracle which modern psychic people call Levitation; and he must surely have either been a liar or a literal witness, for there could have been no doubts or degrees about such a prodigy happening to such a person: it must have been like seeing one of the huge pillars of the church suspended like a cloud. Nobody knows, I imagine, what spiritual storm of exaltation or agony produces this convulsion in matter or space; but the thing does almost certainly occur. Even in the case of ordinary Spiritualist mediums, for whatever reason, the evidence is very difficult to refute. But probably the most representative revelation of this side of his life may be found in the celebrated story of the miracle of the crucifix; when in the stillness of the church of St. Dominic in Naples, a voice spoke from the carven Christ, and told the kneeling Friar that he had written rightly, and offered him the choice of a reward among all the things of the world.

Not all, I think, have appreciated the point of this particular story as applied to this particular saint. It is an old story, in so far as it is simply the offer made to a devotee of solitude or simplicity, of the pick of all the prizes of life. The hermit, true or false, the fakir, the fanatic or the cynic, Stylites on his column or Diogenes in his tub, can all be pictured as tempted by the powers of the earth, of the air or of the heavens, with the offer of the best of everything; and replying that they want nothing. In the Greek cynic or stoic it really meant the mere negative; that he wanted nothing. In the Oriental mystic or fanatic, it sometimes meant a sort of positive negative; that he wanted Nothing; that Nothing was really what he wanted. Sometimes it expressed a noble independence, and the twin virtues of antiquity, the love of liberty and the hatred of luxury. Sometimes it only expressed a self-sufficiency that is the very opposite of sanctity. But even the stories of real saints, of this sort, do not quite cover the case of St. Thomas. He was not a person who wanted nothing;

and he was a person who was enormously interested in everything. His answer is not so inevitable or simple as some may suppose. As compared with many other saints, and many other philosophers, he was avid in his acceptance of Things; in his hunger and thirst for Things. It was his special spiritual thesis that there really are things; and not only the Thing; that the Many existed as well as the One. I do not mean things to eat or drink or wear, though he never denied to these their place in the noble hierarchy of Being; but rather things to think about, and especially things to prove, to experience and to know. Nobody supposes that Thomas Aquinas, when offered by God his choice among all the gifts of God, would ask for a thousand pounds, or the Crown of Sicily, or a present of rare Greek wine. But he might have asked for things that he really wanted: and he was a man who could want things; as he wanted the lost manuscript of St. Chrysostom. He might have asked for the solution of an old difficulty; or the secret of a new science; or a flash of the inconceivable intuitive mind of the angels, or any one of a thousand things that would really have satisfied his broad and virile appetite for the very vastness and variety of the universe. The point is that for him, when the voice spoke from between the outstretched arms of the Crucified, those arms were truly opened wide, and opening most gloriously the gates of all the worlds; they were arms pointing to the east and to the west, to the ends of the earth and the very extremes of existence. They were truly spread out with a gesture of omnipotent generosity; the Creator himself offering Creation itself; with all its millionfold mystery of separate beings, and the triumphal chorus of the creatures. That is the blazing background of multitudinous Being that gives the particular strength, and even a sort of surprise, to the answer of St. Thomas, when he lifted at last his head and spoke with, and for, that almost blasphemous audacity which is one with the humility of his religion; "I will have Thyself."

Or, to add the crowning and crushing irony to this story, so uniquely Christian for those who can really understand it, there are some who feel that the audacity is softened by insisting that he said, "*Only* Thyself."

Of these miracles, in the strictly miraculous sense, there are not so many as in the lives of less immediately influential saints; but they are probably pretty well authenticated; for he was a well-known public man in a prominent position, and, what is even more convenient for him, he had any number of highly incensed enemies, who could be trusted to sift his claims. There is at least one miracle of healing; that of a woman who touched his gown; and several incidents that may be variants of the story of the crucifix at Naples. One of these stories, however, has a further importance as bringing us to another section of his more private, personal or even emotional religious life; the section that expressed itself in poetry. When he was stationed at Paris, the other Doctors of the Sorbonne put before him a problem about the nature of the mystical change in the elements of the Blessed Sacrament, and he proceeded to write, in his customary manner, a very careful and elaborately lucid statement of his own solution. Needless to say he felt with hearty simplicity the heavy responsibility and gravity of such a judicial decision; and not unnaturally seems to have worried about it more than he commonly did over his work. He sought for guidance in more than usually prolonged prayer and intercession; and finally, with one of those few but striking bodily gestures that mark the turning points of his life, he threw down his thesis at the foot of the crucifix on the altar, and left it lying there; as if awaiting judgment. Then he turned and came down the altar steps and buried himself once more in prayer; but the other Friars, it is said, were watching; and well they might be. For they declared afterwards that the figure of Christ had come down from the cross before their mortal eyes; and stood upon the scroll, saying "Thomas, thou hast written well concerning the Sacrament of My Body." It was after this vision that the incident is said to have happened, of his being born up miraculously in mid-air.

An acute observer said of Thomas Aquinas in his own time, "He could alone restore all philosophy, if it had been burnt by fire." That is what is meant by saying that he was an original man, a creative mind; that he could have made his own cosmos out of stones and straws, even without the manuscripts of Aristotle or Augustine. But there is here a not uncommon confusion, between the thing in which a man is most original and that in which he is most interested; or between the thing that he does best and the thing that he loves most. Because St. Thomas was a unique and striking philosopher, it is almost unavoidable that this book should be merely, or mainly, a sketch of his philosophy. It cannot be, and does not pretend to be, a sketch of his theology. But this is because the theology of a saint is simply the theism of a saint; or rather the theism of all saints. It is less individual, but it is much more intense. It is concerned with the common origin; but it is hardly an occasion for originality. Thus we are forced to think first of Thomas as the maker of the Thomist philosophy; as we think first of Christopher Columbus as the discoverer of America, though he may have been quite sincere in his pious hope to convert the Khan of Tartary; or of James Watt as the discoverer of the steam-engine, though he may have been a devout fire-worshipper, or a sincere Scottish Calvinist, or all kinds of curious things. Anyhow, it is but natural that Augustine and Aquinas, Bonaventure and Duns Scotus, all the doctors and the saints, should draw nearer to each other as they approach the divine units in things; and that there should in that sense be less difference between them in theology than in philosophy. It is true that, in some matters, the critics of Aquinas thought his philosophy had unduly affected his theology. This is especially so, touching the charge that he made the state of Beatitude too intellectual, conceiving it as the satisfaction of the love of truth; rather than specially as the truth of love. It is true that the mystics and the men of the Franciscan school, dwelt more lovingly on the admitted supremacy of love. But it was mostly a matter of emphasis; perhaps tinged faintly by temperament, possibly (to suggest something which is easier to feel than to explain), in the case of St. Thomas, a shadowy influence of a sort of shyness. Whether the supreme ecstasy is more affectional than intellectual is no very deadly matter of quarrel among men who believe it is both, but do not profess even to imagine the actual experience of either. But I have a sort of feeling that, even if St. Thomas had thought it was as emotional as St. Bonaventure did, he would never have been so emotional about it. It would always have embarrassed him to write about love at such length.

The one exception permitted to him was the rare but remarkable output of his poetry. All sanctity is secrecy; and his sacred poetry was really a secretion; like the pearl in a very tightly closed oyster. He may have written more of it than we know; but part of it came into public use through the particular circumstance of his being asked to compose the office for the Feast of Corpus Christi: a festival first established after the controversy to which he had contributed, in the scroll that he laid on the altar. It does certainly reveal an entirely different side of his genius; and it certainly was genius. As a rule, he was an eminently practical prose writer; some would say a very prosaic prose writer. He maintained controversy with an eye on only two qualities; clarity and courtesy. And he maintained these because they were entirely practical qualities; affecting the probabilities of conversion. But the composer of the Corpus Christi service was not merely what even the wild and woolly would call a poet; he was what the most fastidious would call an artist. His double function rather recalls the double activity of some great Renaissance craftsman, like Michelangelo or Leonardo da Vinci, who would work on the outer wall, planning and building the fortifications of the city; and then retire into the inner chamber to carve or model some cup or casket for a reliquary. The Corpus Christi Office is like some old musical instrument, quaintly and carefully inlaid with many coloured stones and metals; the author has gathered remote texts about pasture and fruition like rare herbs; there is a notable lack of the loud and obvious in the harmony; and the whole is strung with two strong Latin lyrics. Father John O'Connor has translated them with an almost miraculous aptitude; but a good translator will be the first to agree that no translation is good; or, at any rate, good enough. How are we to find eight short English words which actually stand for "*Sumit unus, sumunt mille; quantum isti, tantum ille*"? How is anybody really to render the sound of the "*Pange Lingua*," when the very first syllable has a clang like the clash of cymbals?

There was one other channel, besides that of poetry, and it was that of private affections, by which this large and shy man could show that he had really as much *Caritas* as St. Francis; and certainly as much as any Franciscan theologian. Bonaventure was not likely to think that Thomas was lacking in the love of God, and certainly he was never lacking in the love of Bonaventure. He felt for his whole family a steady, we might say a stubborn tenderness; and, considering how his family treated him, this would seem to call not only for charity, but for his characteristic virtue of patience. Towards the end of his life, he seems to have leaned especially on his love of one of the brethren, a Friar named Reginald, who received from him some strange and rather startling confidences, of the kind that he very seldom gave even to his friends. It was to Reginald that he gave that last and rather extraordinary hint, which was the end of his controversial career, and practically of his earthly life; a hint that history has never been able to explain.

He had returned victorious from his last combat with Siger of Brabant; returned and retired. This particular quarrel was the one point, as we may say, in which his outer and his inner life had crossed and coincided; he realised how he had longed from childhood to call up all allies in the battle for Christ; how he had only long afterwards called up Aristotle as an ally; and now in that last nightmare of sophistry, he had for the first time truly realised that some might really wish Christ to go down before Aristotle. He never recovered from the shock. He won his battle, because he was the best brain of his time, but he could not forget such an inversion of the whole idea and purpose of his life. He was the sort of man who hates hating people. He had not been used to hating even their hateful ideas, beyond a certain point. But in the abyss of anarchy opened by Siger's sophistry of the Double Mind of Man, he had seen the possibility of the perishing of all idea of religion, and even of all idea of truth. Brief and fragmentary as are the phrases that record it, we can gather that he came back with a sort of horror of that outer world, in which there blew such wild winds of doctrine, and a longing for the inner world which any Catholic can share, and in which the saint is not cut off from simple men. He resumed the strict routine of religion, and for some time said nothing to anybody. And then something happened (it is said while he was celebrating Mass) the nature of which will never be known among mortal men.

His friend Reginald asked him to return also to his equally regular habits of reading and writing, and following the controversies of the hour. He said with a singular emphasis, "I can write no more." There seems to have been a silence; after which Reginald again ventured to approach the subject; and Thomas answered him with even greater vigour, "I can write no more. I have seen things which make all my writings like straw."

In 1274, when Aquinas was nearly fifty, the Pope, rejoicing in the recent victory over the Arabian sophists, sent word to him, asking him to come to a Council on these controversial matters, to be held at Lyons. He rose in automatic obedience, as a soldier rises; but we may fancy that there was something in his eyes that told those around him that obedience to the outer command would not in fact frustrate obedience to some more mysterious inner command; a signal that only he had seen. He set out with his friend on the journey, proposing to rest for the night with his sister, to whom he was deeply devoted; and when he came into her house he was stricken down with some unnamed malady. We need not discuss the doubtful medical problems. It is true that he had always been one of those men, healthy in the main, who are overthrown by small illnesses; it is equally true that there is no very clear account of this particular illness. He was eventually taken to a monastery at Fossanuova; and his strange end came upon him with great strides. It may be worth remarking, for those who think that he thought too little of the emotional or romantic side of religious truth, that he asked to have The Song of Solomon read through to him from beginning to end. The feelings of the men about him must have been mingled and rather indescribable; and certainly quite different from his own. He confessed his sins and he received his God; and we may be sure that the great philosopher had entirely forgotten philosophy. But it was not entirely so with those who had loved him, or even those who merely lived in his time. The elements of the narrative are so few, yet so essential, that we have a strong sense in reading the story of the two emotional sides of the event. Those men must have known that a great mind was still labouring like a great mill in the midst of them. They must have felt that, for that moment, the inside of the monastery was larger than the outside. It must have resembled the case of some mighty modern engine, shaking the ramshackle building in which it is for the moment enclosed. For truly that machine was made of the wheels of all the worlds; and revolved like that cosmos of concentric spheres which, whatever its fate in the face of changing science, must always be something of a symbol for philosophy; the depth of double and triple transparencies more mysterious than darkness; the sevenfold, the terrible crystal. In the world of that mind there was a wheel of angels, and a wheel of planets, and a wheel of plants or of animals; but there was also a just and intelligible order of all earthly things, a sane authority and a self-respecting liberty, and a hundred answers to a hundred questions in the complexity of ethics or economics. But there must have been a moment, when men knew that the thunderous mill of thought had stopped suddenly; and that after the shock of stillness that wheel would shake the world no more; that there was nothing now within that hollow house but a great hill of clay; and the confessor, who had been with him in the inner chamber, ran forth as if in fear, and whispered that his confession had been that of a child of five.

CHAPTER VI

THE APPROACH TO THOMISM

The fact that Thomism is the philosophy of common sense is itself a matter of common sense. Yet it wants a word of explanation, because we have so long taken such matters in a very uncommon sense. For good or evil, Europe since the Reformation, and most especially England since the Reformation, has been in a peculiar sense the home of paradox. I mean in the very peculiar sense that paradox was at home, and that men were at home with it. The most familiar example is the English boasting that they are practical *because* they are not logical. To an ancient Greek or a Chinaman this would seem exactly like saying that London clerks excel in adding up their ledgers, because they are not accurate in their arithmetic. But the point is not that it is a paradox; it is that parodoxy has become orthodoxy; that men repose in a paradox as placidly as in a platitude. It is not that the practical man stands on his head, which may sometimes be a stimulating if startling gymnastic; it is that he *rests* on his head; and even sleeps on his head. This is an important point, because the use of paradox is to awaken the mind. Take a good paradox, like that of Oliver Wendell Holmes: "Give us the luxuries of life and we will dispense with the necessities." It is amusing and therefore arresting; it has a fine air of defiance; it contains a real if romantic truth. It is all part of the fun that it is stated almost in the form of a contradiction in terms. But most people would agree that there would be considerable danger in basing the whole social system on the notion that necessities are not necessary; as some have based the whole British Constitution on the notion that nonsense will always work out as common sense. Yet even here, it might be said that the invidious example has spread, and that the modern industrial system does really say, "Give us luxuries like coal-tar soap, and we will dispense with necessities like corn."

So much is familiar; but what is not even now realised is that not only the practical politics, but the abstract philosophies of the modern world have had this queer twist. Since the modern world began in the sixteenth century, nobody's system of philosophy has really corresponded to everybody's sense of reality: to what, if left to themselves, common men would call common sense. Each started with a paradox: a peculiar point of view demanding the sacrifice of what they would call a sane point of view. That is the one thing common to Hobbes and Hegel, to Kant and Bergson. to Berkeley and William James. A man had to believe something that no normal man would believe, if it were suddenly propounded to his simplicity; as that law is above right, or right is outside reason, or things are only as we think them, or everything is relative to a reality that is not there. The modern philosopher claims, like a sort of confidence man, that if once we will grant him this, the rest will be easy; he will straighten out the world, if once he is allowed to give this one twist to the mind.

It will be understood that in these matters I speak as a fool; or, as our democratic cousins would say, a moron; anyhow as a man in the street; and the only object of this chapter is to show that the Thomist philosophy is nearer than most philosophies to the mind of the man in the street. I am not, like Father D'Arcy, whose admirable book on St. Thomas has illuminated many problems for me, a trained philosopher, acquainted with the technique of the trade. But I hope Father D'Arcy will forgive me if I take one example from his book, which exactly illustrates what I mean. He, being a trained philosopher, is naturally trained to put up with philosophers. Also, being a trained priest, he is naturally accustomed, not only to suffer fools gladly, but (what is sometimes even harder) to suffer clever people gladly. Above all, his wide reading in metaphysics has made him patient with clever people when they indulge in folly. The consequence is that he can write calmly and even blandly sentences like these. "A certain likeness can be detected between the aim and method of St. Thomas and those of Hegel. There are, however, also remarkable differences. For St. Thomas it is impossible that contradictories should exist together, and again reality and intelligibility correspond, but a thing must first be, to be intelligible."

Let the man in the street be forgiven, if he adds that the "remarkable difference" seems to him to be that St. Thomas was sane and Hegel was mad. The moron refuses to admit that Hegel can both exist and not exist; or that it can be possible to understand Hegel, if there is no Hegel to understand. Yet Father D'Arcy mentions this Hegelian paradox as if it were all in the day's work; and of course it is, if the work is reading all the modern philosophers as searchingly and sympathetically as he has done. And this is what I mean saying that all modern philosophy starts with a stumbling-block. It is surely not too much to say that there *seems* to be a twist, in saying that contraries are not incompatible; or that a thing can "be" intelligible and not as yet "be" at all.

Against all this the philosophy of St. Thomas stands founded on the universal common conviction that eggs are eggs. The Hegelian may say that an egg is really a hen, because it is a part of an endless process of Becoming; the Berkeleian may hold that poached eggs only exist as a dream exists; since it is quite as easy to call the dream the cause of the eggs as the eggs the cause of the dream; the Pragmatist may believe that we get the best out of scrambled eggs by forgetting that they ever were eggs, and only remembering the scramble. But no pupil of St. Thomas needs to addle his brains in order adequately to addle his eggs; to put his head at any peculiar angle in looking at eggs, or squinting at eggs, or winking the other eye in order to see a new simplification of eggs. The Thomist stands in the broad daylight of the brotherhood of men, in their common consciousness that eggs are not hens or dreams or mere practical assumptions; but things attested by the Authority of the Senses, which is from God.

Thus, even those who appreciate the metaphysical depth of Thomism in other matters have expressed surprise that he does not deal at all with what many now think the main metaphysical question; whether we can prove that the primary act of recognition of any reality is real. The answer is that St. Thomas recognised instantly, what so many modern sceptics have begun to suspect rather laboriously; that a man must either answer that question in the affirmative, or else never answer any question, never ask any question, never even exist intellectually, to answer or to ask. I suppose it is true in a sense that a man can be a fundamental sceptic, but he cannot be anything else: certainly not even a defender of fundamental scepticism. If a man feels that all the movements of his own mind are meaningless, then his mind is meaningless, and he is meaningless; and it does not mean anything to attempt to discover his meaning. Most fundamental sceptics appear to survive, because they are not consistently sceptical and not at all fundamental. They will first deny everything and then admit something, if for the sake of argument—or often rather of attack without argument. I saw an almost startling example of this essential frivolity in a professor of final scepticism, in a paper the other day. A man wrote to say that he accepted nothing but Solipsism, and added that he had often wondered it was not a more common philosophy. Now Solipsism simply means that a man believes in his own existence, but not in anybody or anything else. And it never struck this simple sophist, that if his philosophy was true, there obviously were no other philosophers to profess it.

To this question "Is there anything?" St. Thomas begins by answering "Yes"; if he began by answering "No", it would not be the beginning, but the end. That is what some of us call common sense. Either there is no philosophy, no philosophers, no thinkers, no thought, no anything; or else there is a real bridge between the mind and reality. But he is actually less exacting than many thinkers, much less so than most rationalist and materialist thinkers, as to what that first step involves; he is content, as we shall see, to say that it involves the recognition of Ens or Being as something definitely beyond ourselves. Ens is Ens: Eggs are eggs, and it is not tenable that all eggs were found in a mare's nest.

Needless to say, I am not so silly as to suggest that all the writings of St. Thomas are simple and straightforward; in the sense of being easy to understand. There are passages I do not in the least understand myself; there are passages that puzzle much more learned and logical philosophers than I am; there are passages about which the greatest Thomists still differ and dispute. But that is a question of a thing being hard to read or understand: not hard to accept when understood. That is a mere matter of "The Cat sat on the Mat" being written in Chinese characters: or "Mary had a Little Lamb" in Egyptian hieroglyphics. The only point I am stressing here is that Aquinas is almost always on the side of simplicity, and supports the ordinary man's acceptance of ordinary truisms. For instance, one of the most obscure passages, in my very inadequate judgment, is that in which he explains how the mind is certain of an external object and not merely of an impression of that object; and yet apparently reaches it through a concept, though not merely through an impression. But the only point here is that he does explain that the mind is certain of an external object. It is enough for this purpose that his conclusion is what is called the conclusion of common sense; that it is his purpose to justify common sense; even though he justifies it in a passage which happens to be one of rather uncommon subtlety. The problem of later philosophers is that their conclusion is as dark as their demonstration; or that they bring out a result of which the result is chaos.

Unfortunately, between the man in the street and the Angel of the Schools, there stands at this moment a very high brick wall, with spikes on the top, separating two men who in many ways stand for the same thing. The wall is almost a historical accident; at least it was built a very long time ago, for reasons that need not affect the needs of normal men today; least of all the greatest need of normal men; which is for a normal philosophy. The first difficulty is merely a difference of form; not in the medieval but in the modern sense. There is first a simple obstacle of language; there is then a rather more subtle obstacle of logical method. But the language itself counts for a great deal; even when it is translated, it is still a foreign language; and it is, like other foreign languages, very often translated wrong. As with every other literature from another age or country, it carried with it an atmosphere which is beyond the mere translation of words, as they are translated in a traveller's phrase-book. For instance, the whole system of St. Thomas hangs on one huge and yet simple idea; which does actually cover everything there is, and even everything that could possibly be. He represents this cosmic conception by the word *Ens*; and anybody who can read any Latin at all, however rudely, feels it to be the apt and fitting word; exactly as he feels it in a French word in a piece of good French prose. It ought to be a matter of logic; but it is also a matter of language.

Unfortunately there is no satisfying translation of the word *Ens*. The difficulty is rather verbal than logical, but it is practical. I mean that when the translator says in English 'being', we are aware of a rather different atmosphere. Atmosphere ought not to affect these absolutes of the intellect; but it does. The new psychologists, who are almost eagerly at war with reason, never tire of telling us that the very terms we use are coloured by our subconsciousness, with something we meant to exclude from our consciousness. And one need not be so idealistically irrational as a modern psychologist, in order to admit that the very shape and sound of words do make a difference, even in the baldest prose, as they do in the most beautiful poetry. We cannot quite prevent the imagination from remembering irrelevant associations even in the abstract sciences like mathematics. Jones Minimus, hustled from history to geometry, may for an instant connect the Angles of the isosceles triangle with the Angles of the Anglo-Saxon Chronicle; and even the mature mathematician, if he is as mad as the psychoanalyst hopes, may have in the roots of his subconscious mind something material in his idea of a root. Now it unfortunately happens that the word 'being', as it comes to a modern Englishman, through modern associations, has a sort of hazy atmosphere that is not in the short and sharp Latin word. Perhaps it reminds him of fantastic professors in fiction, who wave their hands and say, "Thus do we mount to the ineffable heights of pure and radiant Being:" or, worse still, of actual professors in real life, who say, "All Being is Becoming; and is but the evolution of Not-Being by the law of its Being." Perhaps it only reminds him of romantic rhapsodies in old love stories; "Beautiful and adorable being, light and breath of my very being." Anyhow it has a wild and woolly sort of sound; as if only very vague people used it; or as if it might mean all sorts of different things.

Now the Latin word *Ens* has a sound like the English word *End.* It is final and even abrupt; it is nothing except itself. There was once a silly gibe against Scholastics like Aquinas, that they discussed whether angels could stand on the point of a needle. It is at least certain that this first word of Aquinas is as sharp as the point of a pin. For that also is, in an almost ideal sense, an End. But when we say that St. Thomas Aquinas is concerned fundamentally with the idea of Being, we must not admit any of the cloudier generalisations that we may have grown used to, or even grown tired of, in the sort of idealistic writing that is rather rhetoric than philosophy. Rhetoric is a very fine thing in its place, as a medieval scholar would have willingly agreed, as he taught it along with logic in the schools; but St. Thomas Aquinas himself is not at all rhetorical. Perhaps he is hardly even sufficiently rhetorical. There are any number of purple patches in Augustine; but there are no purple patches in Aquinas. He did on certain definite occasions drop into poetry; but he very seldom dropped into oratory. And so little was he in touch with some modern tendencies, that whenever he did write poetry, he actually put it into poems. There is another side to this, to be noted later. He very specially possessed the philosophy that inspires poetry; as he did so largely inspire Dante's poetry. And poetry without philosophy has only inspiration, or, in vulgar language, only wind. He had, so to speak, the imagination without the imagery. And even this is perhaps too sweeping. There is an image of his, that is true poetry as well as true philosophy; about the tree of life bowing down with a huge humility, because of the very load of its living fruitfulness; a thing Dante might have described so as to overwhelm us with the tremendous twilight and almost drug us with the divine fruit. But normally, we may say that his words are brief even when his books are long. I have taken the example of the word *Ens*, precisely because it is one of the cases in which Latin is plainer than plain English. And his style, unlike that of St. Augustine and many Catholic Doctors, is always a penny plain rather than twopence coloured. It is often difficult to understand, simply because the subjects are so difficult that hardly any mind, except one like his own, can fully understand them. But he never darkens it by using words without knowledge, or even more legitimately, by using words belonging only to imagination or intuition. So far as his method is concerned, he is perhaps the one real Rationalist among all the children of men.

This brings us to the other difficulty; that of logical method. I have never understood why there is supposed to be something crabbed or antique about a syllogism; still less can I understand what any-body means by talking as if induction had somehow taken the place of deduction. The whole point of deduction is that true premises produce a true conclusion. What is called induction seems simply to mean collecting a larger number of true premises. or perhaps, in some physical matters, taking rather more trouble to see that they are true. It may be a fact that a modern man can get more out of a great many premises, concerning microbes or asteroids than a medieval man could get out of a very few premises about salamanders and unicorns. But the process of deduction from the data is the same for the modern mind as for the medieval mind; and what is pompously called induction is simply collecting more of the data. And Aristotle or Aquinas, or anybody in his five wits, would of course agree that the conclusion could only be true if the premises were true; and that the more true premises there were the better. It was the misfortune of medieval culture that there were not enough true premises, owing to the rather ruder conditions of travel or experiment. But however perfect were the conditions of travel or experiment, they could only produce premises; it would still be necessary to deduce conclusions. But many modern people talk as if what they call induction were some magic way of reaching a conclusion, without using any of those horrid old syllogisms. But induction does not lead us to a conclusion. Induction only leads us to a deduction. Unless the last three syllogistic steps are all right, the conclusion is all wrong. Thus, the great nineteenth century men of science, whom I was brought up to revere ("accepting the conclusions of science," it was always called), went out and closely inspected the air and the earth, the chemicals and the gases, doubtless more closely than Aristotle or Aquinas, and then came back and embodied their final conclusion in a syllogism. "All matter is made of microscopic little knobs which are indivisible. My body is made of matter. Therefore my body is made of microscopic little knobs which are indivisible." They were not wrong in the form of their reasoning; because it is the only way to reason. In this world there is nothing except a syllogism—and a fallacy. But of course these modern men knew, as the medieval men knew, that their conclusions would not be true unless their premises were true. And that is where the trouble began. For the men of science, or their sons and nephews, went out and took another look at the knobby nature of matter; and were surprised to find that it was not knobby at all. So they came back and completed the process with their syllogism; "All matter is made of whirling protons and electrons. My body is made of matter. Therefore my body is made of whirling protons and electrons." And that again is a good syllogism; though they may have to look at matter once or twice more, before we know whether it is a true premise and a true conclusion. But in the final process of truth there is nothing else except a good syllogism. The only other thing is a bad syllogism; as in the familiar fashionable shape; "All matter is made of protons and electrons. I should very much like to think that mind is much the same as matter. So I will announce, through the microphone or the megaphone, that my mind is made of protons and electrons." But that is not induction; it is only a very bad blunder in deduction. That is not another or new way of thinking; it is only ceasing to think.

What is really meant, and what is much more reasonable, is that the old syllogists sometimes set out the syllogism at length; and certainly that is not always necessary. A man can run down the three steps much more quickly than that; but a man cannot run down the three steps if they are not there. If he does, he will break his neck, as if he walked out of a fourth-story window. The truth about this false antithesis of induction and deduction is simply this; that as premises or data accumulated, the emphasis and detail was shifted to them, from the final deduction to which they lead. But they did lead to a final deduction; or else they led to nothing. The logician had so much to say about electrons or microbes that he dwelt most on these data and shortened or assumed his ultimate syllogism. But if he reasoned rightly, however rapidly, he reasoned syllogistically.

As a matter of fact, Aquinas does not usually argue in syllogisms; though he always argues syllogistically. I mean he does not set out all the steps of the logic in each case; the legend that he does so is part of that loose and largely unverified legend of the Renaissance; that the Schoolmen were all crabbed and mechanical medieval bores. But he does argue with a certain austerity, and disdain of ornament, which may make him seem monotonous to anyone specially seeking the modern forms of wit or fancy. But all this has nothing to do with the question asked at the beginning of this chapter and needing to be answered at the end of it; the question of what he is arguing for. In that respect it can be repeated, most emphatically, that he is arguing for common sense.

He is arguing for a common sense which would even now commend itself to most of the common people. He is arguing for the popular proverbs that seeing is believing; that the proof of the pudding is in the eating; that a man cannot jump down his own throat or deny the fact of his own existence. He often maintains the view by the use of abstractions; but the abstractions are no more abstract than Energy or Evolution or Space-Time; and they do not land us, as the others often do, in hopeless contradictions about common life. The Pragmatist sets out to be practical, but his practicality turns out to be entirely theoretical. The Thomist begins by being theoretical, but his theory turns out to be entirely practical. That is why a great part of the world is returning to it today.

Finally, there is some real difficulty in the fact of a foreign language; apart from the ordinary fact of the Latin language. Modern philosophical terminology is not always exactly identical with plain English; and medieval philosophical terminology is not at all identical even with modern philosophical terminology. It is not really very difficult to learn the meaning of the main terms; but their medieval meaning is sometimes the exact opposite of their modern meaning. The obvious example is in the pivotal word "form." We say nowadays, "I wrote a formal apology to the Dean," or "The proceedings when we wound up the Tip-Cat Club were purely formal." But we mean that they were purely fictitious; and St. Thomas, had he been a member of the Tip-Cat Club, would have meant just the opposite. He would have meant that the proceedings dealt with the very heart and soul and secret of the whole being of the Tip-Cat Club; and that the apology to the Dean was so essentially apologetic that it tore the very heart out in tears of true contrition. For "formal" in Thomist language means actual, or possessing the real decisive quality that makes a thing itself. Roughly when he describes a thing as made out of Form and Matter, he very rightly recognises that Matter is the more mysterious and indefinite and featureless element; and that what stamps anything with its own identity is its Form. Matter, so to speak, is not so much the solid as the liquid or gaseous thing in the cosmos: and in this most modern scientists are beginning to agree with him. But the form is the fact; it is that which makes a brick a brick, and a bust a bust, and not the shapeless and trampled clay of which either may be made. The stone that broke a statuette, in some Gothic niche, might have been itself a statuette; and under chemical analysis, the statuette is only a stone. But such a chemical analysis is entirely false as a philosophical analysis. The reality, the thing that makes the two things real, is in the idea of the image and in the idea of the image-breaker. This is only a passing example of the mere idiom of the Thomist terminology; but it is not a bad prefatory specimen of the truth of Thomist thought. Every artist knows that the form is not superficial but fundamental; that the form is the foundation. Every sculptor knows that the form of the statue is not the outside of the statue, but rather the inside of the statue; even in the sense of the inside of the sculptor. Every poet knows that the sonnet-form is not only the form of the poem; but the poem. No modern critic who does not understand what the medieval Schoolman meant by form can meet the Schoolman as an intellectual equal.

CHAPTER VII

THE PERMANENT PHILOSOPHY

It is a pity that the word Anthropology has been degraded to the study of Anthropoids. It is now incurably associated with squabbles between prehistoric professors (in more senses than one) about whether a chip of stone is the tooth of a man or an ape; sometimes settled as in that famous case, when it was found to be the tooth of a pig. It is very right that there should be a purely physical science of such things; but the name commonly used might well, by analogy, have been dedicated to things not only wider and deeper, but rather more relevant. Just as, in America, the new Humanists have pointed out to the old Humanitarians that their humanitarianism has been largely concentrated on things that are *not* specially human, such as physical conditions, appetites, economic needs, environment and so on— so in practice those who are called Anthropologists have to narrow their minds to the materialistic things that are not notably anthropic. They have to hunt through history and pre-history something which emphatically is not *Homo Sapiens*, but is always in fact regarded as *Simius Insipiens*. *Homo Sapiens* can only be considered in relation to *Sapientia* and only a book like that of St. Thomas is really devoted to the intrinsic idea of *Sapientia*. In short, there ought to be a real study called Anthropology corresponding to Theology. In this sense St. Thomas Aquinas, perhaps more than he is anything else, is a great anthropologist.

I apologise for the opening words of this chapter to all those excellent and eminent men of science, who are engaged in the real study of humanity in its relation to biology. But I rather fancy that they will be the last to deny that there has been a somewhat disproportionate disposition, in popular science, to turn the study of human beings into the study of savages. And savagery is not history; it is either the beginning of history or the end of it. I suspect that the greatest scientists would agree that only too many professors have thus been lost in the bush or the jungle; professors who wanted to study anthropology and never got any further than anthropophagy. But I have a particular reason for prefacing this suggestion of a higher anthropology by an apology to any genuine biologists who might seem to be included, but are certainly not included, in a protest against cheap popular science. For the first thing to be said about St. Thomas as an anthropologist, is that he is really remarkably like the best sort of modern biological anthropologist; of the sort who would call themselves Agnostics. This fact is so sharp and decisive a turning point in history, that the history really needs to be recalled and recorded.

St. Thomas Aquinas closely resembles the great Professor Huxley, the Agnostic who invented the word Agnosticism. He is like him in his way of starting the argument, and he is unlike everybody else, before and after, until the Huxleyan age. He adopts almost literally the Huxleyan definition of the Agnostic method; "To follow reason as far as it will go;" the only question is—where does it go? He lays down the almost startlingly modern or materialist statement; "Every thing that is in the intellect has been in the senses." This is where he began, as much as any modern man of science, nay, as much as any modern materialist who can now hardly be called a man of science; at the very opposite end of enquiry from that of the mere mystic. The Platonists, or at least the Neo-Platonists, all tended to the view that the mind was lit entirely from within; St. Thomas insisted that it was lit by five windows, that we call the windows of the senses. But he wanted the light from without to shine on what was within. He wanted to study the nature of Man, and not merely of such moss and mushrooms as he might see through the window, and which he valued as the first enlightening experience of man. And starting from this point, he proceeds to climb the House of Man, step by step and story by story, until he has come out on the highest tower and beheld the largest vision.

In other words, he is an anthropologist, with a complete theory of Man, right or wrong. Now the modern Anthropologists, who called themselves Agnostics, completely failed to be Anthropologists at all. Under their limitations, they could not get a complete theory of Man, let alone a complete theory of nature. They began by ruling out something which they called the Unknowable. The incomprehensibility was almost comprehensible, if we could really understand the Unknowable in the sense of the Ultimate. But it rapidly became apparent that all sorts of things were Unknowable, which were exactly the things that a man has got to know. It is necessary to know whether he is responsible or irresponsible, perfect or imperfect, perfectible or unperfectible, mortal or immortal, doomed or free, not in order to understand God, but in order to understand Man. Nothing that leaves these things under a cloud of religious doubt can possibly pretend to be a Science of Man; it shrinks from anthropology as completely as from theology. Has a man free will; or is his sense of choice an illusion? Has he a conscience, or has his conscience any authority; or is it only the prejudice of the tribal past? Is there real hope of settling these things by human reason; and has *that* any authority? Is he to regard death as final; and is he to regard miraculous help as possible? Now it is all nonsense to say that these are unknowable in any remote sense, like the distinction between the Cherubim and the Seraphim, or the Procession of the Holy Ghost. The Schoolmen may have shot too far beyond our limits in pursuing the Cherubim and Seraphim. But in asking whether a man can choose or whether a man will die, they were asking ordinary questions in natural history; like whether a cat can scratch or whether a dog can smell. Nothing calling itself a complete Science of Man can shirk them. And the great Agnostics did shirk them. They may have said they had no scientific evidence; in that case they failed to produce even a scientific hypothesis. What they generally did produce was a wildly unscientific contradiction. Most Monist moralists simply said that Man has no choice; but he must think and act heroically as if he had. Huxley made morality, and even Victorian morality, in the exact sense, supernatural. He said it had arbitrary rights above nature; a sort of theology without theism.

I do not know for certain why St. Thomas was called the Angelic Doctor: whether it was that he had an angelic temper, or the intellectuality of an Angel; or whether there was a later legend that he concentrated on Angels—especially on the points of needles. If so, I do not quite understand how this idea arose; history has many examples of an irritating habit of labelling somebody in connection with something, as if he never did any thing else. Who was it who began the inane habit of referring to Dr. Johnson as "our lexicographer;" as if he never did anything but write a dictionary? Why do most people insist on meeting the large and far-reaching mind of Pascal at its very narrowest point: the point at which it was sharpened into a spike by the spite of the Jansenists against the Jesuits? It is just possible, for all I know, that this labelling of Aquinas as a specialist was an obscure depreciation of him as a universalist. For that is a very common trick for the belittling of literary or scientific men. St. Thomas must have made a certain number of enemies, though he hardly ever treated them as enemies. Unfortunately, good temper is sometimes more irritating than bad temper. And he had, after all, done a great deal of damage, as many medieval men would have thought; and, what is more curious, a great deal of damage to both sides. He had been a revolutionist against Augustine and a traditionalist against Averrhoes. He might appear to some to have tried to wreck that ancient beauty of the city of God, which bore some resemblance to the Republic of Plato. He might appear to others to have inflicted a blow on the advancing and levelling forces of Islam, as dramatic as that of Godfrey storming Jerusalem. It is possible that these enemies, by wax of damning with faint praise, talked about his very respectable little work on Angels: as a man might say that Darwin was really reliable when writing on coral-insects; or that some of Milton's Latin poems were very creditable indeed. But this is only a conjecture, and many other conjectures are possible. And I am disposed to think that St. Thomas really was rather specially interested in the nature of Angels, for the same reason that made him even more interested in the nature of Men. It was a part of that strong personal interest in things subordinate and semidependent, which runs through his whole system: a hierarchy of higher and lower liberties. He was interested in the problem of the Angel, as he was interested in the problem of the Man, because it was a problem; and especially because it was a problem of an intermediate creature. I do not pretend to deal here with this mysterious quality, as he conceives it to exist in that inscrutable intellectual being, who is less than God but more than Man. But it was this quality of a link in the chain, or a rung in the ladder, which mainly concerned the theologian, in developing his own particular theory of degrees. Above all, it is this which chiefly moves him, when he finds so fascinating the central mystery of Man. And for him the point is always that Man is not a balloon going up into the sky nor a mole burrowing merely in the earth; but rather a thing like a tree whose roots are fed from the earth, while its highest branches seem to rise almost to the stars.

I have pointed out that mere modern free-thought has left everything in a fog, including itself. The assertion that thought is free led first to the denial that will is free; but even about that there was no real determination among the Determinists. In practice, they told men that they must treat their will as free though it was not free. In other words, Man must live a double life; which is exactly the old heresy of Siger of Brabant about the Double Mind. In other words, the nineteenth century left everything in chaos: and the importance of Thomism to the twentieth century is that it may give us back a cosmos. We can give here only the rudest sketch of how Aquinas, like the Agnostics, beginning in the cosmic cellars, yet climbed to the cosmic towers.

Without pretending to span within such limits the essential Thomist idea, I may be allowed to throw out a sort of rough version of the fundamental question, which I think I have known myself, consciously or unconsciously since my childhood. When a child looks out of the nursery window and sees anything, say the green lawn of the garden, what does he actually know; or does he know anything? There are all sorts of nursery games of negative philosophy played round this question. A brilliant Victorian scientist delighted in declaring that the child does not see any grass at all; but only a sort of green mist reflected in a tiny mirror of the human eye. This piece of rationalism has always struck me as almost insanely irrational. If he is not sure of the existence of the grass, which he sees through the glass of a window, how on earth can he be sure of the existence of the retina, which he sees through the glass of a microscope? If sight deceives, why can it not go on deceiving? Men of another school answer that grass is a mere green impression on the mind; and that he can be sure of nothing except the mind. They declare that he can only be conscious of his own consciousness; which happens to be the one thing that we know the child is not conscious of at all. In that sense, it would be far truer to say that there is grass and no child, than to say that there is a conscious child but no grass. St. Thomas Aquinas, suddenly intervening in this nursery quarrel, says emphatically that the child is aware of *Ens*. Long before he knows that grass is grass, or self is self, he knows that something is something. Perhaps it would be best to say very emphatically (with a blow on the table), "There *is* an Is." That is as much monkish credulity as St. Thomas asks of us at the start. Very few unbelievers start by asking us to believe so little. And yet, upon this sharp pin-point of reality, he rears by long logical processes that have never really been successfully overthrown, the whole cosmic system of Christendom.

Thus, Aquinas insists very profoundly but very practically, that there *instantly* enters, with this idea of affirmation the idea of contradiction. It is instantly apparent, even to the child, that there cannot be both affirmation and contradiction. Whatever you call the thing he sees, a moon or a mirage or a sensation or a state of consciousness, when he sees it, he knows it is not true that he does not see it. Or whatever you call what he is supposed to be doing, seeing or dreaming or being conscious of an impression, he knows that if he is doing it, it is a lie to say he is not doing it. Therefore there has already entered *something* beyond even the first fact of being; there follows it like its shadow the first fundamental creed or commandment, that a thing cannot be and not be. Henceforth, in common or popular language, there is a false and true. I say in popular language, because Aquinas is nowhere more subtle than in pointing out that being is not strictly the same as truth; seeing truth must mean the appreciation of being by some mind capable of appreciating it. But in a general sense there has entered that primeval world of pure actuality, the division and dilemma that brings the ultimate sort of war into the world; the everlasting duel between Yes and No. This is the dilemma that many sceptics have darkened the universe and dissolved the mind solely in order to escape. They are those who maintain that there is something that is both Yes and No. I do not know whether they pronounce it Yo.

The next step following on this acceptance of actuality or certainty, or whatever we call it in popular language, is much more difficult to explain in that language. But it represents exactly the point at which nearly all other systems go wrong, and in taking the third step abandon the first. Aquinas has affirmed that our first sense of fact is a fact; and he cannot go back on it without falsehood. But when we come to look at the fact or facts, as we know them, we observe that they have a rather queer character; which has made many moderns grow strangely and restlessly sceptical about them. For instance, they are largely in a state of change, from being one thing to being another; or their qualities are relative to other things; or they appear to move incessantly; or they appear to vanish entirely. At this point, as I say, many sages lose hold of the first principle of reality, which they would concede at first; and fall back on saying that there is nothing except change; or nothing except comparison; or nothing except flux; or in effect that there is nothing at all. Aquinas turns the whole argument the other way, keeping in line with his first realisation of reality. There is no doubt about the being of being, even if it does sometimes look like becoming; that is because what we see is not the fullness of being; or (to continue a sort of colloquial slang) we never see being being as much as it can. Ice is melted into cold water and cold water is heated into hot water; it cannot be all three at once. But this does not make water unreal or even relative; it only means that its being is limited to being one thing at a time. But the fullness of being is everything that it can be; and without it the lesser or approximate forms of being cannot be explained as anything; unless they are explained away as nothing.

This crude outline can only at the best be historical rather than philosophical. It is impossible to compress into it the metaphysical proofs of such an idea; especially in the medieval metaphysical language. But this distinction in philosophy is tremendous as a turning point in history. Most thinkers, on realising the apparent mutability of being, have really forgotten their own realisation of the being, and believed only in the mutability. They cannot even say that a thing changes into another thing; for them there is no instant in the process at which it is a thing at all. It is only a change. It would be more logical to call it nothing changing into nothing, than to say (on these principles) that there ever was or will be a moment when the thing is itself. St. Thomas maintains that the ordinary thing at any moment is something; but it is not everything that it could be. There is a fullness of being, in which it could be everything that it can be. Thus, while most sages come at last to nothing but naked change, he comes to the ultimate thing that is unchangeable, because it is all the other things at once. While they describe a change which is really a change in nothing, he describes a changelessness which includes the changes of everything. Things change because they are not complete; but their reality can only be explained as part of something that is complete. It is God.

Historically, at least, it was round this sharp and crooked corner that all the sophists have followed each other while the great Schoolman went up the high road of experience and expansion; to the beholding of cities, to the building of cities. They all failed at this early stage because, in the words of the old game, they took away the number they first thought of. The recognition of something, of a thing or things, is the first act of the intellect. But because the examination of a thing shows it is not a fixed or final thing, they inferred that there is nothing fixed or final. Thus, in various ways, they all began to see a thing as something thinner than a thing; a wave; a weakness; an abstract instability. St. Thomas, to use the same rude figure, saw a thing that was thicker than a thing; that was even more solid than the solid but secondary facts he had started by admitting as facts. Since we know them to be real, any elusive or bewildering element in their reality cannot really be unreality; and must be merely their relation to the real reality. A hundred human philosophies, ranging over the earth from Nominalism to Nirvana and Maya, from formless evolution to mindless quietism, all come from this first break in the Thomist chain; the notion that, because what we see does not satisfy us or explain itself, it is not even what we see. That cosmos is a contradiction in terms and strangles itself; but Thomism cuts itself free. The defect we see, in what is, is simply that it is not all that is. God is more actual even than Man; more actual even than Matter; for God with all His powers at every instant is immortally in action.

A cosmic comedy of a very curious sort occurred recently; involving the views of very brilliant men, such as Mr. Bernard Shaw and the Dean of St. Paul's. Briefly, freethinkers of many sorts had often said they had no need of a Creation, because the cosmos had always existed and always would exist. Mr. Bernard Shaw said he had become an atheist because the universe had gone on making itself from the beginning or without a beginning; Dean Inge later displayed consternation at the very idea that the universe could have an end. Most modern Christians, living by tradition where medieval Christians could live by logic or reason, vaguely felt that it was a dreadful idea to deprive them of the Day of Judgment. Most modern agnostics (who are delighted to have their ideas called dreadful) cried out all the more, with one accord, that the self-producing, self-existent, truly scientific universe had never needed to have a beginning and could not come to an end. At this very instant, quite suddenly, like the look-out man on a ship who shouts a warning about a rock, the *real* man of science, the expert who was examining the facts, announced in a loud voice that the universe *was* coming to an end. He had not been listening, of course, to the talk of the amateurs; he had been actually examining the texture of matter; and he said it was disintegrating: the world was apparently blowing itself up by a gradual explosion called energy; the whole business would certainly have an end and had presumably had a beginning. This was very shocking indeed; not to the orthodox, but rather specially to the unorthodox; who are rather more easily shocked. Dean Inge, who had been lecturing the orthodox for years on their stern duty of accepting all scientific discoveries, positively wailed aloud over this truly tactless scientific discovery; and practically implored the scientific discoverers to go away and discover something different. It seems almost incredible; but it is a fact that he asked what God would have to amuse Him, if the universe ceased. That is a measure of how much the modern mind needs Thomas Aquinas. But even without Aquinas, I can hardly conceive any educated man, let alone such a learned man, believing in God at all without assuming that God contains in Himself every perfection including eternal joy; and does not require the solar system to entertain him like a circus.

To step out of these presumptions, prejudices and private disappointments, into the world of St. Thomas, is like escaping from a scuffle in a dark room into the broad daylight. St. Thomas says, quite straightforwardly, that he himself believes this world has a beginning and end; because such seems to be the teaching of the Church; the validity of which mystical message to mankind he defends elsewhere with dozens of quite different arguments. Anyhow, the Church said the world would end; and apparently the Church was right; always supposing (as we are always supposed to suppose) that the latest men of science are right. But Aquinas says he sees no particular reason, in reason, why this world should not be a world without end; or even without beginning. And he is quite certain that, if it were entirely without end or beginning, there would still be exactly the same logical need of a Creator. Anybody who does not see that, he gently implies, does not really understand what is meant by a Creator.

For what St. Thomas means is not a medieval picture of an old king; but this second step in the great argument about *Ens* or Being; the second point which is so desperately difficult to put correctly in popular language. That is why I have introduced it here in the particular form of the argument that there must be a Creator even if there is no Day of Creation. Looking at Being as it is now, as the baby looks at the grass, we see a second thing about it; in quite popular language, it *looks* secondary and dependent. Existence exists; but it is not sufficiently self-existent; and would never become so merely by going on existing. The same primary sense which tells us it is Being, tells us that it is not perfect Being; not merely imperfect in the popular controversial sense of containing sin or sorrow; but imperfect as Being; less actual than the actuality it implies. For instance, its Being is often only Becoming; beginning to Be or ceasing to Be; it implies a more constant or complete thing of which it gives in itself no example. That is the meaning of that basic medieval phrase, "Everything that is moving is moved by another;" which, in the clear subtlety of St. Thomas, means inexpressibly more than the mere Deistic "somebody wound up the clock" with which it is probably often confounded. Anyone who thinks deeply will see that motion has about it an essential incompleteness, which approximates to something more complete.

The actual argument is rather technical; and concerns the fact that potentiality does not explain itself; moreover, in any case, unfolding must be of something folded. Suffice it to say that the mere modern evolutionists, who would ignore the argument do not do so because they have discovered any flaw in the argument; for they have never discovered the argument itself. They do so because they are too shallow to see the flaw in their own argument for the weakness of their thesis is covered by fashionable phraseology, as the strength of the old thesis is covered by old-fashioned phraseology. But for those who really think, there is always something really unthinkable about the whole evolutionary cosmos, as they conceive it; because it is something coming out of nothing; an ever-increasing flood of water pouring out of an empty jug. Those who can simply accept that, without even seeing the difficulty, are not likely to go so deep as Aquinas and see the solution of his difficulty. In a word, the world does not explain itself, and cannot do so merely by continuing to expand itself. But anyhow it is absurd for the Evolutionist to complain that it is unthinkable for an admittedly unthinkable God to make everything out of nothing and then pretend that it is *more* thinkable that nothing should turn itself into everything.

We have seen that most philosophers simply fail to philosophise about things because they change; they also fail to philosophise about things because they differ. We have no space to follow St. Thomas through all these negative heresies; but a word must be said about Nominalism or the doubt founded on the things that differ. Everyone knows that the Nominalist declared that things differ too much to be really classified; so that they are only labelled. Aquinas was a firm but moderate Realist, and therefore held that there really are general qualities; as that human beings are human, amid other paradoxes. To be an extreme Realist would have taken him too near to being a Platonist. He recognized that individuality is real, but said that it coexists with a common character making some generalisation possible; in fact, as in most things, he said exactly what all common sense would say, if no intelligent heretics had ever disturbed it. Nevertheless, they still continue to disturb it. I remember when Mr. H. G. Wells had an alarming fit of Nominalist philosophy; and poured forth book after book to argue that everything is unique and untypical as that a man is so much an individual that he is not even a man. It is a quaint and almost comic fact, that this chaotic negation especially attracts those who are always complaining of social chaos, and who propose to replace it by the most sweeping social regulations. It is the very men who say that nothing can be classified, who say that everything must be codified. Thus Mr. Bernard Shaw said that the only golden rule is that there is no golden rule. He prefers an iron rule; as in Russia.

But this is only a small inconsistency in some moderns as individuals. There is a much deeper inconsistency in them as theorists in relation to the general theory called Creative Evolution. They seem to imagine that they avoid the metaphysical doubt about mere change by assuming (it is not very clear why) that the change will always be for the better. But the mathematical difficulty of finding a corner in a curve is not altered by turning the chart upside down, and saying that a downward curve is now an upward curve. The point is that there is no point in the curve; no place at which we have a logical right to say that the curve has reached its climax, or revealed its origin, or come to its end. It makes no difference that they choose to be cheerful about it, and say, "It is enough that there is always a beyond;" instead of lamenting, like the more realistic poets of the past, over the tragedy of mere Mutability. It is not enough that there is always a beyond; because it might be beyond bearing. Indeed the only defence of this view is that sheer boredom is such an agony, that any movement is a relief. But the truth is that they have never read St. Thomas, or they would find, with no little terror, that they really agree with him. What they really mean is that change is not mere change; but is the unfolding of something; and if it is thus unfolded, though the unfolding takes twelve million years, it must be there already. In other words, they agree with Aquinas that there is everywhere potentiality that has not reached its end in act. But if it is a definite potentiality, and if it can only end in a definite act, why then there is a Great Being, in whom all potentialities already exist as a plan of action. In other words, it is impossible even to say that the change is for the better, unless the best exists somewhere, both before and after the change. Otherwise it is indeed mere change, as the blankest sceptics or the blackest pessimists would see it. Suppose two entirely new paths open before the progress of Creative Evolution. How is the evolutionist to know which Beyond is the better; unless he accepts from the past and present some standard of the best? By their superficial theory everything can change; everything can improve, even the nature of improvement. But in their submerged common sense, they do not really think that an ideal of kindness could change to an ideal of cruelty. It is typical of them that they will sometimes rather timidly use the word Purpose; but blush at the very mention of the word Person.

St. Thomas is the very reverse of anthropomorphic, in spite of his shrewdness as an anthropologist. Some theologians have even claimed that he is too much of an agnostic; and has left the nature of God too much of an intellectual abstraction. But we do not need even St. Thomas, we do not need anything but our own common sense, to tell us that if there has been from the beginning anything that can possibly be called a Purpose, it must reside in something that has the essential elements of a Person. There cannot be an intention hovering in the air all by itself, any more than a memory that nobody remembers or a joke that nobody has made. The only chance for those supporting such suggestions is to take refuge in blank and bottomless irrationality; and even then it is impossible to prove that anybody has any right to be unreasonable, if St. Thomas has no right to be reasonable.

In a sketch that aims only at the baldest simplification, this does seem to me the simplest truth about St. Thomas the philosopher. He is one, so to speak, who is faithful to his first love; and it is love at first sight. I mean that he immediately recognised a real quality in things; and afterwards resisted all the disintegrating doubts arising from the nature of those things. That is why I emphasise, even in the first few pages, the fact that there is a sort of purely Christian humility and fidelity underlying his philosophic realism. St. Thomas could as truly say, of having seen merely a stick or a stone, what St. Paul said of having seen the rending of the secret heavens, "I was not disobedient to the heavenly vision." For though the stick or the stone is an earthly vision, it is through them that St. Thomas finds his way to heaven; and the point is that he is obedient to the vision; he does not go back on it. Nearly all the other sages who have led or misled mankind do, on one excuse or another, go back on it. They dissolve the stick or the stone in chemical solutions of scepticism; either in the medium of mere time and change; or in the difficulties of classification of unique units; or in the difficulty of recognising variety while admitting unity. The first of these three is called debate about flux or formless transition; the second is the debate about Nominalism and Realism, or the existence of general ideas; the third is called the ancient metaphysical riddle of the One and the Many. But they can all be reduced under a rough image to this same statement about St. Thomas. He is still true to the first truth and refusing the first treason. He will not deny what he has seen, though it be a secondary and diverse reality. He will not take away the numbers he first thought of, though there may be quite a number of them.

He has seen grass; and will not say he has not seen grass, because it today is and tomorrow is cast into the oven. That is the substance of all scepticism about change, transition, transformism and the rest. He will not say that there is no grass but only growth. If grass grows and withers, it can only mean that it is part of a greater thing, which is even more real; not that the grass is less real than it looks. St. Thomas has a really logical right to say, in the words of the modern mystic, A. E.: "I begin by the grass to be bound again to the Lord."

He has seen grass and grain; and he will not say that they do not differ, because there is something common to grass and grain. Nor will he say that there is nothing common to grass and grain, because they do really differ. He will not say, with the extreme Nominalists, that because grain can be differentiated into all sorts of fruitage, or grass trodden into mire with any kind of weed, therefore there can be no*classification* to distinguish weeds from slime or to draw a fine distinction between cattle-food and cattle. He will not say with the extreme Platonists, on the other hand, that he saw the perfect fruit in his own head by shutting his eyes, *before* he saw any difference between grain and grass. He saw one thing and then another thing and then a common quality; but he does not really pretend that he saw the quality before the thing.

He has seen grass and gravel; that is to say, he has seen things really different; things not classified together like grass and grains. The first flash of fact shows us a world of really strange things not merely strange to us, but strange to each other. The separate things need have nothing in common except Being. Everything is Being; but it is not true that everything is Unity. It is here, as I have said, that St. Thomas does definitely one might say defiantly, part company with the Pantheist and Monist. All things are; but among the things that are is the thing called difference, quite as much as the thing called similarity. And here again we begin to be bound again to the Lord, not only by the universality of grass, but by the incompatibility of grass and gravel. For this world of different and varied beings is especially the world of the Christian Creator; the world of created things, like things made by an artist; as compared with the world that is only one thing, with a sort of shimmering and shifting veil of misleading change; which is the conception of so many of the ancient religions of Asia and the modern sophistries of Germany. In the face of these, St. Thomas still stands stubborn in the same obstinate objective fidelity. He has seen grass and gravel; and he is not disobedient to the heavenly vision.

To sum up; the reality of things, the mutability of things, the diversity of things, and all other such things that can be attributed to things, is followed carefully by the medieval philosopher, without losing touch with the original point of the reality. There is no space in this book to specify the thousand steps of thought by which he shows that he is right. But the point is that, even apart from being right he is real. He is a realist in a rather curious sense of his own, which is a third thing, distinct from the almost contrary medieval and modern meanings of the word. Even the doubts and difficulties about reality have driven him to believe in more reality rather than less. The *deceitfulness* of things which has had so sad an effect on so many sages, has almost a contrary effect on this sage. If things deceive us, it is by being more real than they seem. As ends in themselves they always deceive us; but as things tending to a greater end, they are even more real than we think them. If they seem to have a relative unreality (so to speak) it is because they are potential and not actual; they are unfulfilled, like packets of seeds or boxes of fireworks. They have it in them to be more real than they are. And there is an upper world of what the Schoolman called Fruition, or Fulfilment, in which all this relative relativity becomes actuality; in which the trees burst into flower or the rockets into flame.

Here I leave the reader, on the very lowest rung of those ladders of logic, by which St. Thomas besieged and mounted the House of Man. It is enough to say that by arguments as honest and laborious, he climbed up to the turrets and talked with angels on the roofs of gold. This is, in a very rude outline, his philosophy; it is impossible in such an outline to describe his theology. Anyone writing so small a book about so big a man, must leave out something. Those who know him best will best understand why, after some considerable consideration, I have left out the only important thing.

CHAPTER VIII

THE SEQUEL TO ST. THOMAS

It is often said that St. Thomas, unlike St. Francis, did not permit in his work the indescribable element of poetry. As, for instance, that there is little reference to any pleasure in the actual flowers and fruit of natural things, though any amount of concern with the buried roots of nature. And yet I confess that, in reading his philosophy, I have a very peculiar and powerful impression analogous to poetry. Curiously enough, it is in some ways more analogous to painting, and reminds me very much of the effect produced by the best of the modern painters, when they throw a strange and almost crude light upon stark and rectangular objects, or seem to be groping for rather than grasping the very pillars of the subconscious mind. It is probably because there is in his work a quality which is Primitive, in the best sense of a badly misused word; but anyhow, the pleasure is definitely not only of the reason, but also of the imagination.

Perhaps the impression is connected with the fact that painters deal with things without words. An artist draws quite gravely the grand curves of a pig; because he is not thinking of the *word* pig. There is no thinker who is so unmistakably thinking about things and not being misled by the indirect influence of words, as St. Thomas Aquinas. It is true in that sense that he has not the advantage of words, any more than the disadvantage of words. Here he differs sharply, for instance, from St. Augustine who was, among other things a wit. He was also a sort of prose poet, with a power over words in their atmospheric and emotional aspect; so that his books abound with beautiful passages that rise in the memory like strains of music; the *illi in vos saeviant*; or the unforgettable cry, "Late I have loved thee, O Ancient Beauty!" It is true that there is little or nothing of this kind in St. Thomas; but if he was without the higher uses of the mere magic of words, he was also free from that abuse of it, by mere sentimentalists or self-centred artists, which can become merely morbid and a very black magic indeed. And truly it is by some such comparison with the purely introspective intellectual that we may find a hint about the real nature of the thing I describe, or rather fail to describe; I mean the elemental and primitive poetry that shines through all his thoughts; and especially through the thought with which all his thinking begins. It is the intense rightness of his sense of the relation between the mind and the real thing outside the mind.

That *strangeness* of things, which is the light in all poetry, and indeed in all art, is really connected with their otherness; or what is called their objectivity. What is subjective must be stale; it is exactly what is objective that is in this imaginative manner strange. In this the great contemplative is the complete contrary of that false contemplative, the mystic who looks only into his own soul, the selfish artist who shrinks from the world and lives only in his own mind. According to St. Thomas, the mind acts freely of itself, but its freedom exactly consists in finding a way out to liberty and the light of day; to reality and the land of the living. In the subjectivist, the pressure of the world forces the imagination inwards. In the Thomist, the energy of the mind forces the imagination outwards, but because the images it seeks are real things. All their romance and glamour, so to speak, lies in the fact that they are real things; things *not* to be found by staring inwards at the mind. The flower is a vision because it is not only a vision. Or, if you will, it is a vision because it is not a dream. This is for the poet the strangeness of stones and trees and solid things; they are strange because they are solid. I am putting it first in the poetical manner, and indeed it needs much more technical subtlety to put it in the philosophical manner. According to Aquinas, the object becomes a part of the mind; nay, according to Aquinas, the mind actually becomes the object. But, as one commentator acutely puts it, it only becomes the object and does not create the object. In other words, the object *is* an object; it can and does exist outside the mind, or in the absence of the mind. And *therefore* it enlarges the mind of which it becomes a part. The mind conquers a new province like an emperor; but only because the mind has answered the bell like a servant. The mind has opened the doors and windows, because it is the natural activity of what is inside the house to find out what is outside the house. If the mind is sufficient to itself, it is insufficient for itself. For this feeding upon fact *is* itself; as an organ it has an object which is objective; this eating of the strange strong meat of reality.

Note how this view avoids both pitfalls; the alternative abysses of impotence. The mind is not merely receptive, in the sense that it absorbs sensations like so much blotting-paper; on that sort of softness has been based all that cowardly materialism, which conceives man as wholly servile to his environment. On the other hand, the mind is not purely creative, in the sense that it paints pictures on the windows and then mistakes them for a landscape outside. But the mind is active, and its activity consists in following, so far as the will chooses to follow, the light outside that does really shine upon real landscapes. That is what gives the indefinably virile and even adventurous quality to this view of life; as compared with that which holds that material inferences pour in upon an utterly helpless mind, or that which holds that psychological influences pour out and create an entirely baseless phantasmagoria. In other words, the essence of the Thomist common sense is that two agencies are at work; reality and the recognition of reality; and their meeting is a sort of marriage. Indeed it is very truly a marriage, because it is fruitful; the only philosophy now in the world that really is fruitful. It produces practical results, precisely because it is the combination of an adventurous mind and a strange fact.

M. Maritain has used an admirable metaphor, in his book *Theonas*, when he says that the external fact *fertilises* the internal intelligence, as the bee fertilises the flower. Anyhow, upon that marriage, or whatever it may be called, the whole system of St. Thomas is founded; God made Man so that he was capable of coming in contact with reality; and those whom God hath joined, let no man put asunder.

Now, it is worthy of remark that it is the only working philosophy. Of nearly all other philosophies it is strictly true that their followers work in spite of them, or do not work at all. No sceptics work sceptically; no fatalists work fatalistically; all without exception work on the principle that it is possible to assume what it is not possible to believe. No materialist who thinks his mind was made up for him, by mud and blood and heredity, has any hesitation in making up his mind. No sceptic who believes that truth is subjective has any hesitation about treating it as objective.

Thus St. Thomas' work has a constructive quality absent from almost all cosmic systems after him. For he is already building a house, while the newer speculators are still at the stage of testing the rungs of a ladder, demonstrating the hopeless softness of the unbaked bricks, chemically analysing the spirit in the spirit-level, and generally quarrelling about whether they can even make the tools that will make the house. Aquinas is whole intellectual aeons ahead of them, over and above the common chronological sense of saying a man is in advance of his age; he is ages in advance of our age. For he has thrown out a bridge across the abyss of the first doubt, and found reality beyond and begun to build on it. Most modern philosophies are not philosophy but philosophic doubt; that is, doubt about whether there can be any philosophy. If we accept St. Thomas's fundamental act or argument in the acceptance of reality, the further deductions from it will be equally real; they will be things and not words. Unlike Kant and most of the Hegelians, he has a faith that is not merely a doubt about doubt. It is not merely what is commonly called a faith about faith; it is a faith about fact. From this point he can go forward, and deduce and develop and decide, like a man planning a city and sitting in a judgment-seat. But never since that time has any thinking man of that eminence thought that there is any real evidence for anything, not even the evidence of his senses, that was strong enough to bear the weight of a definite deduction.

From all this we may easily infer that this philosopher does not merely touch on social things, or even take them in his stride to spiritual things; though that is always his direction. He takes hold of them, he has not only a grasp of them, but a grip. As all his controversies prove, he was perhaps a perfect example of the iron hand in the velvet glove. He was a man who always turned his full attention to anything; and he seems to fix even passing things as they pass. To him even what was momentary was momentous. The reader feels that any small point of economic habit or human accident is for the moment almost scorched under the converging rays of a magnifying lens. It is impossible to put in these pages a thousandth part of the decisions on details of life that may be found in his work; it would be like reprinting the law-reports of an incredible century of just judges and sensible magistrates. We can only touch on one or two obvious topics of this kind.

I have noted the need to use modern atmospheric words for certain ancient atmospheric things; as in saying that St. Thomas was what most modern men vaguely mean by an Optimist. In the same way, he was very much what they vaguely mean by a Liberal. I do not mean that any of his thousand political suggestions would suit any such definite political creed; if there are nowadays any definite political creeds. I mean, in the same sense, that he has a sort of atmosphere of believing in breadth and balance and debate. He may not be a Liberal by the extreme demands of the moderns for we seem always to mean by the moderns the men of the last century, rather than this. He was very much of a Liberal compared with the most modern of all moderns for they are nearly all of them turning into Fascists and Hitlerites. But the point is that he obviously preferred the sort of decisions that are reached by deliberation rather than despotic action; and while, like all his contemporaries and coreligionists, he has no doubt that true authority may be authoritative, he is rather averse to the whole savour of its being arbitrary. He is much less of an Imperialist than Dante, and even his Papalism is not very Imperial. He is very fond of phrases like "a mob of free men" as the essential material of a city; and he is emphatic upon the fact that law, when it ceases to be justice, ceases even to be law.

If this work were controversial, whole chapters could be given to the economics as well as the ethics of the Thomist system. It would be easy to show that, in this matter, he was a prophet as well as a philosopher. He foresaw from the first the peril of that mere reliance on trade and exchange, which was beginning about his time; and which has culminated in a universal commercial collapse in our time. He did not merely assert that Usury is unnatural, though in saying that he only followed Aristotle and obvious common sense, which was never contradicted by anybody until the time of the commercialists, who have involved us in the collapse. The modern world began by Bentham writing the Defence of Usury, and it has ended after a hundred years in even the vulgar newspaper opinion finding Finance indefensible. But St. Thomas struck much deeper than that. He even mentioned the truth, ignored during the long idolatry of trade, that things which men produce only to sell are likely to be worse in quality than the things they produce in order to consume. Something of our difficulty about the fine shades of Latin will be felt when we come to his statement that there is always a certain *inhonestas* about trade. For *inhonestas* does not exactly mean dishonesty. It means approximately "something unworthy," or, more nearly perhaps, "something not quite handsome." And he was right; for trade, in the modern sense, does mean selling something for a little more than it is worth, nor would the nineteenth century economists have denied it. They would only have said that he was not practical; and this seemed sound while their view led to practical prosperity. Things are a little different now that it has led to universal bankruptcy.

Here, however, we collide with a colossal paradox of history. The Thomist philosophy and theology, quite fairly compared with other philosophies like the Buddhist or the Monist, with other theologies like the Calvinist or the Christian Scientist, is quite obviously a working and even a fighting system; full of common sense and constructive confidence; and therefore normally full of hope and promise. Nor is this hope vain or this promise unfulfilled. In this not very hopeful modern moment, there are no men so hopeful as those who are today looking to St. Thomas as a leader in a hundred crying questions of craftsmanship and ownership and economic ethics. There is undoubtedly a hopeful and creative Thomism in our time. But we are none the less puzzled by the fact that this did not immediately follow on St. Thomas's time. It is true that there was a great march of progress in the thirteenth century; and in some things, such as the status of the peasant, matters had greatly improved by the end of the Middle Ages. But nobody can honestly say that Scholasticism had greatly improved by the end of the Middle Ages. Nobody can tell how far the popular spirit of the Friars had helped the later popular medieval movements; or how far this great Friar, with his luminous rules of justice and his lifelong sympathy with the poor, may have indirectly contributed to the improvement that certainly occurred. But those who followed his method, as distinct from his moral spirit, degenerated with a strange rapidity; and it was certainly not in the Scholastics that the improvement occurred. Of some of the Scholastics we can only say that they took every thing that was worst in Scholasticism and made it worse. They continued to count the steps of logic; but every step of logic took them further from common sense. They forgot how St. Thomas had started almost as an agnostic; and seemed resolved to leave nothing in heaven or hell about which anybody could be agnostic. They were a sort of rabid rationalists, who would have left no mysteries in the Faith at all. In the earliest Scholasticism there is something that strikes a modern as fanciful and pedantic; but, properly understood, it has a fine spirit in its fancy. It is the spirit of freedom; and especially the spirit of free will. Nothing seems more quaint, for instance, than the speculations about what would have happened to every vegetable or animal or angel, if Eve had chosen *not* to eat the fruit of the tree. But this was originally full of the thrill of choice; and the feeling that she might have chosen otherwise. It was this detailed detective method that was followed, without the thrill of the original detective story. The world was cumbered with countless tomes, proving by logic a thousand things that can be known only to God. They developed all that was really sterile in Scholasticism, and left for us all that is really fruitful in Thomism.

There are many historical explanations. There is the Black Death, which broke the back of the Middle Ages; the consequent decline in clerical culture, which did so much to provoke the Reformation. But I suspect that there was another cause also; which can only be stated by saying that the contemporary fanatics, who controverted with Aquinas, left their own school behind them; and in a sense that school triumphed after all. The really narrow Augustinians, the men who saw the Christian life only as the narrow way, the men who could not even comprehend the great Dominican's exultation in the blaze of Being, or the glory of God in all his creatures, the men who continued to insist feverishly on every text, or even on every truth, that appeared pessimistic or paralysing, these gloomy Christians could not be extirpated from Christendom; and they remained and waited for their chance. The narrow Augustinians, the men who would have no science or reason or rational use of secular things, might have been defeated in controversy, but they had an accumulated passion of conviction. There was an Augustinian monastery in the North where it was near to explosion.

Thomas Aquinas had struck his blow; but he had not entirely settled the Manichees. The Manichees are not so easily settled; in the sense of settled forever. He had insured that the main outline of the Christianity that has come down to us should be supernatural but not anti-natural; and should never be darkened with a false spirituality to the oblivion of the Creator and the Christ who was made Man. But as his tradition trailed away into less liberal or less creative habits of thought, and as his medieval society fell away and decayed through other causes, the thing against which he had made war crept back into Christendom. A certain spirit or element in the Christian religion, necessary and sometimes noble but always needing to be balanced by more gentle and generous elements in the Faith, began once more to strengthen, as the framework of Scholasticism stiffened or split. The Fear of the Lord, that is the beginning of wisdom, and therefore belongs to the beginnings, and is felt in the first cold hours before the dawn of civilisation; the power that comes out of the wilderness and rides on the whirlwind and breaks the gods of stone; the power before which the eastern nations are prostrate like a pavement; the power before which the primitive prophets run naked and shouting, at once proclaiming and escaping from their god; the fear that is rightly rooted in the beginnings of every religion true or false: the fear of the Lord, that is the beginning of wisdom; but not the end.

It is often remarked as showing the ironical indifference of rulers to revolutions, and especially the frivolity of those who are called the Pagan

Popes of the Renaissance, in their attitude to the Reformation, that when the Pope first heard of the first movements of Protestantism, which had started in Germany, he only said in an offhand manner that it was "some quarrel of monks." Every Pope of course was accustomed to quarrels among the monastic orders; but it has always been noted as a strange and almost uncanny negligence that he could see no more than this in the beginnings of the great sixteenth century schism. And yet, in a somewhat more recondite sense, there is something to be said for what he has been blamed for saying. In one sense, the schismatics had a sort of spiritual ancestry even in mediaeval times.

It will be found earlier in this book; and it *was* a quarrel of monks. We have seen how the great name of Augustine, a name never mentioned by Aquinas without respect but often mentioned without agreement covered an Augustinian school of thought naturally lingering longest in the Augustinian Order. The difference, like every difference between Catholics, was only a difference of emphasis. The Augustinians stressed the idea of the impotence of man before God, the omniscience of God about the destiny of man, the need for holy fear and the humiliation of intellectual pride, more than the opposite and corresponding truths of free will or human dignity or good works. In this they did in a sense continue the distinctive note of St. Augustine, who is even now regarded as relatively the determinist doctor of the Church. But there is emphasis and emphasis; and a time was coming when emphasising the one side was to mean flatly contradicting the other. Perhaps, after all, it did begin with a quarrel of monks; but the Pope was yet to learn how quarrelsome a monk could be. For there was one particular monk in that Augustinian monastery in the German forests, who may be said to have had a single and special talent for emphasis; for emphasis and nothing except emphasis; for emphasis with the quality of earthquake. He was the son of a slatecutter; a man with a great voice and a certain volume of personality; brooding, sincere, decidedly morbid; and his name was Martin Luther. Neither Augustine nor the Augustinians would have desired to see the day of that vindication of the Augustinian tradition; but in one sense, perhaps, the Augustinian tradition was avenged after all.

It came out of its cell again, in the day of storm and ruin, and cried out with a new and mighty voice for an elemental and emotional religion, and for the destruction of all philosophies. It had a peculiar horror and loathing of the great Greek philosophies, and of the scholasticism that had been founded on those philosophies. It had one theory that was the destruction of all theories; in fact it had its own theology which was itself the death of theology. Man could say nothing to God, nothing from God, nothing about God, except an almost inarticulate cry for mercy and for the supernatural help of Christ, in a world where all natural things were useless. Reason was useless. Will was useless. Man could not move himself an inch any more than a stone. Man could not trust what was in his head any more than a turnip. Nothing remained in earth or heaven, but the name of Christ lifted in that lonely imprecation; awful as the cry of a beast in pain.

We must be just to those huge human figures, who are in fact the hinges of history. However strong, and rightly strong, be our own controversial conviction, it must never mislead us into thinking that something trivial has transformed the world. So it is with that great Augustinian monk, who avenged all the ascetic Augustinians of the Middle Ages; and whose broad and burly figure has been big enough to block out for four centuries the distant human mountain of Aquinas. It is not, as the moderns delight to say, a question of theology. The Protestant theology of Martin Luther was a thing that no modern Protestant would be seen dead in a field with; or if the phrase be too flippant, would be specially anxious to touch with a barge-pole. That Protestantism was pessimism; it was nothing but bare insistence on the hopelessness of all human virtue, as an attempt to escape hell. That Lutheranism is now quite unreal; more modern phases of Lutheranism are rather more unreal; but Luther was not unreal. He was one of those great elemental barbarians, to whom it is indeed given to change the world. To compare those two figures hulking so big in history, in any philosophical sense, would of course be futile and even unfair. On a great map like the mind of Aquinas, the mind of Luther would be almost invisible. But it is not altogether untrue to say, as so many journalists have said without caring whether it was true or untrue, that Luther opened an epoch; and began the modern world.

He was the first man who ever consciously used his consciousness or what was later called his Personality. He had as a fact a rather strong personality. Aquinas had an even stronger personality; he had a massive and magnetic presence; he had an intellect that could act like a huge system of artillery spread over the whole world; he had that instantaneous presence of mind in debate, which alone really deserves the name of wit. But it never occurred to him to use anything except his wits, in defence of a truth distinct from himself. It never occurred to Aquinas to use Aquinas as a weapon. There is not a trace of his ever using his personal advantages, of birth or body or brain or breeding, in debate with anybody. In short, he belonged to an age of intellectual unconsciousness, to an age of intellectual innocence, which was very intellectual. Now Luther did begin the modern mood of depending on things not merely intellectual. It is not a question of praise or blame; it matters little whether we say that he was a strong personality, or that he was a bit of a big bully. When he quoted a Scripture text, inserting a word that is not in Scripture, he was content to shout back at all hecklers: "Tell them that Dr. Martin Luther will have it so!" That is what we now call Personality. A little later it was called Psychology. After that it was called Advertisement or Salesmanship. But we are not arguing about advantages or disadvantages. It is due to this great Augustinian pessimist to say, not only that he did triumph at last over the

Angel of the Schools, but that he did in a very real sense make the modern world. He destroyed Reason; and substituted Suggestion.

It is said that the great Reformer publicly burned the *Summa Theologica* and the works of Aquinas; and with the bonfire of such books this book may well come to an end. They say it is very difficult to burn a book; and it must have been exceedingly difficult to burn such a mountain of books as the Dominican had contributed to the controversies of Christendom. Anyhow, there is something lurid and apocalyptic about the idea of such destruction, when we consider the compact complexity of all that encyclopaedic survey of social and moral and theoretical things. All the close-packed definitions that excluded so many errors and extremes; all the broad and balanced judgments upon the clash of loyalties or the choice of evils; all the liberal speculations upon the limits of government or the proper conditions of justice; all the distinctions between the use and abuse of private property; all the rules and exceptions about the great evil of war; all the allowances for human weakness and all the provisions for human health; all this mass of medieval humanism shrivelled and curled up in smoke before the eyes of its enemy; and that great passionate peasant rejoiced darkly, because the day of the Intellect was over. Sentence by sentence it burned, and syllogism by syllogism; and the golden maxims turned to golden flames in that last and dying glory of all that had once been the great wisdom of the Greeks. The great central Synthesis of history, that was to have linked the ancient with the modern world, went up in smoke and, for half the world, was forgotten like a vapour.

For a time it seemed that the destruction was final. It is still expressed in the amazing fact that (in the North) modern men can still write histories of philosophy, in which philosophy stops with the last little sophists of Greece and Rome; and is never heard of again until the appearance of such a third-rate philosopher as Francis Bacon. And yet this small book, which will probably do nothing else, or have very little other value, will be at least a testimony to the fact that the tide has turned once more. It is four hundred years after; and this book, I hope (and I am happy to say I believe) will probably be lost and forgotten in the flood of better books about St. Thomas Aquinas, which are at this moment pouring from every printing-press in Europe, and even in England and America. Compared with such books it is obviously a very slight and amateurish production; but it is not likely to be burned, and if it were, it would not leave even a noticeable gap in the pouring mass of new and magnificent work, which is now daily dedicated to the *philosophia perennis*; to the Everlasting Philosophy.